Oc

for F

love from

Lucy +

Mini

A Walker's Guidebook

A WALKER'S GUIDEBOOK

Serendipitous Outings Near New York City
INCLUDING
a Section for Birders

MARINA HARRISON
LUCY D. ROSENFELD

Illustrations by Lucy D. Rosenfeld

MICHAEL KESEND PUBLISHING • NEW YORK

Copyright 1988 © by Lucy D. Rosenfeld & Marina Harrison
First publication 1988

Library of Congress Cataloging-in-Publication Data
Harrison, Marina, 1939-
A walker's guidebook: serendipitous outings near New York City: including a section for birders / Marina Harrison, Lucy D. Rosenfeld.
   p. cm.
   ISBN 0-935576-27-4
1. New York Region—Description and travel—Guide-books.
2. Walking—New York Region—Guide-books. 3. Bird watching —New York Region—Guide-books. I. Rosenfeld, Lucy D., 1939-.
II. Title.
F128. 18.H358 1988
917.4'0443—dc19   88-21608
                                                      CIP

CONTENTS

LONG ISLAND

THE HUDSON VALLEY (EAST)

THE HUDSON VALLEY (WEST)

FOREWORD

This is a book of outings for walkers of every description. We hope that experienced trail hikers, antique-village enthusiasts, nature lovers, adventuresome wanderers, bird watchers, and leisure-time strollers who enjoy conversation, peace, and quiet will all find walks to their taste in this little book. To this end we have compiled a list of outings that includes some of the oddest and prettiest locations, as well as the more traditional natural park sites. All of our walks are well within the abilities of the average family, and some are even easier. A few are for the more rugged hikers, but the views and scenery make them well worth the effort. You'll find outings especially designated for the handicapped and others for people with particular interests: herbs, gravestones, mushrooms, apple picking, fine art, wine making, physical fitness, and beachcombing, among them.

In no way do we pretend that this is a comprehensive guide to all the walks in the New York area. And obviously there are many books designed just for specific interests. What we have tried to do is to offer a collection of outings that will pique the fancy and appeal to many different tastes.

Despite the massive overbuilding of this region, there still are many lovely places to explore. Over a five-year period we have crisscrossed our area, from Long Island to Westchester and Putnam, from New Jersey's seashore to its interior canals, from Connecticut's coast to its colonial villages. We have looked for bird watching sites along the way, and you'll find those we have chosen make for fine walking as well as birding. Our village walking tours are through communities that have managed to retain an architectural identity despite growth and inroads of the 20th century. Each will bring you the aura of a special time or place: a Moravian stone village, a Hudson River landing, a Connecticut Colonial town, a Methodist Victorian camp-village.

While researching these sites we have been encouraged by the sense of preservation that has swept the area. New parklands, gifts of unspoiled greenery and careful conservation of old houses and antique buildings are everywhere. Within a few dozen miles of the city you'll find wonderful, restorative scenery and many un-crowded trails and pathways.

Each of our walks suggests the best time for a hike in the region—and they are not all in the spring! Fall foliage and winter snow walks are included, as are beach and lakeside strolls. We also advise you when *not* to walk in some areas; we prefer un-crowded and solitary strolls and we assume you do too. We also note the difficulty of each hike and designate certain walks as good for small children or for the elderly. You'll find information on parking fees, availability of food and drink, maps, and what to take along (comfortable shoes!), as well as major historic sites and other more touristy things to do after your walk.

The routes we have suggested are generally the shortest; but in some cases we have avoided congested areas by recommending slightly longer, but more pleasant, approaches.

We wish you many pleasant days of walking as we have had, and perhaps the addition to your city life of some new countryish delights. We hope that in most cases you can take your children along on these outings and can show them that a world of serene beauty and of wide-ranging interests awaits them outside the ur-ban scene. And if you're familiar with other nearby special locales that we have missed, please let us know!

We have had a wonderful time working on this book, and we are grateful to the following people for their help and encour-agement: Anne Davidson, Diana A. Green, Judy Kesselman, and . Andy Boose; and to our families, a special thank you.

Lucy D. Rosenfeld and Marina Harrison

NEW JERSEY

1
Walking Through a "Deserted" Village
Allaire State Park

HOW TO GET THERE:

Take Route 80 from the George Washington Bridge, to the Garden State Parkway south to exit 98. (Or, New Jersey Turnpike to Garden State Parkway and exit 11.) Get on Route 195 west. Go to the second exit on 195, which is 31B. Allaire State Park is off Route 524 east; entrance to the park is on the right.

This picturesque spot in Monmouth County was once a bustling iron forge center, known in 1763 as the Williamsburg Forge. By 1822 one Benjamin Howell had joined with a brass founder named James P. Allaire to establish the Howell Works on the site. The village then had 400 people working in bog iron production. (Bog iron ore was produced by decaying vegetation.) The iron was smelted and cast into cauldrons, pots, pipes, stoves, and other objects.

By the mid-19th century, however, higher-grade iron ore in western areas began to drive the forge out of business. Soon Allaire Village lost its manufacturing base, and eventually the entire site was abandoned.

What we see as we walk through is a charming small village, totally uninhabited except for a park ranger station and a general store. The restoration of the old buildings has been careful and is not "hokey." Walking through the village with its widely separated buildings is historically interesting and quite picturesque. The roadway winds through what's left of the village—about 20 buildings—from the old Christ Church (a charming, white New England-style meetinghouse), past the 1835 bakery, the sawmill, the furnace stack, over little bridges, across fields, and into the woods. In addition to the village, there are several nice nature trails. The entire environment re-creates the ambiance of a small rural village surrounded by woods and meadows. Its emptiness and lack of cars, noise, or smoke make it curiously still. And the gentle sloping hillsides with brooks rippling by provide very pleasant country strolling.

The village itself is a small part of a state park. There are trails, camping, and other facilities in the park, which is open officially from May to Labor Day. There is a small parking fee. But you can walk through the village at any time except during January and February. There are tours and other conveniences, such as food, rest rooms, and exhibits, as well as a steam train ride on the Pine Creek Railroad available every day in season and on weekends (except in winter)

If you are taking children along, we recommend visiting the village when many of the facilities are open, for there is a variety of events, such as cider making, fishing contests for children, candle dipping, as well as that steam train ride. Among other events are art shows, concerts, and formal exhibits of quilts, tools, and antique clothing. Call 201-938-3311 for more information.

If, however, you prefer a quieter time or are a walker seeking solitude and natural beauty, visit Allaire out of season; it can get crowded on summer weekends. We visited both in spring and fall, and found it truly a deserted village, in every sense.

The village is open from 10:00 A.M. to 5:00 P.M. Monday to Saturday, and noon to 5:00 Sunday, in season. We hasten to add that "open" does not mean that people are parading around in costumes or providing expensive carriage rides for professional photographers. This is a deserted village in the best sense.

If you wish to leave the village and go off into the wooded trails (much as the last century's citizens must have gone into the nearby forest to find a rabbit for supper), you should bring sturdy wet-shoes. The woods surrounding the village are fairly moist under foot, particularly in spring. You can bring a picnic—there are tables next to the parking area—or in season you can buy refreshments at the visitor's center.

THE WALK

Although tours are available, we liked the self-guided tour, so we could linger as long as we wanted at what we felt were the most interesting spots. You will leave your car at the parking area, and set off, guide map in hand, to your right. There are some 20 buildings—or remains thereof—to be visited, and you can divert your route to the Manasquam Floodplain Trail into the woods, a very pretty nature walk.

Your first stop will be the homes built by Mr. Allaire in about 1832, which now house exhibits and information. You can get a map there. The next building is the foreman's cottage, dating to 1827. Farther along you'll find the entrance to the nature trail, at the bridge over the brook, and the site of the original sawmill. In the grinding mill and screw factory, which employed children of the community, the iron objects were ground and polished.

The grist mill and blacksmith shop from the 1830s are definitely worth a good look, and so is the old bakery, the upstairs of which served as the schoolroom. (James Allaire provided schooling out of his own pocket.) One of the oldest buildings is the manager's home, which was built about 1798 for the stagecoach driver. You'll next come to the Village General Store, which is still in operation and filled with goodies of many kinds. The carpenter shop and enameling building are next along the walk; the exhibits of antique crafts are held in the enameling building.

Soon you'll reach the furnace stack, the most important of Allaire's historic sites, for this is the last of the state's early iron furnaces. It was powered by a waterwheel; today only the stack remains. The dormitory for the workers is one of the original buildings near the furnace. Mr. Allaire himself lived here, as did many workers. The carriage house, hay barn, and cattle barns are next on the route. Finally, you will come to the charming Christ Church, an Episcopalian church dating from the 1830s. There are foundations and remains of other buildings at Allaire, and the interested walker can delve much more deeply into the past of this quintessentially American village by visiting the library and the exhibits.

AFTER THE WALK

Allaire is close to the Atlantic Ocean. In fact, two of the nicest towns on the coast are a short distance away. Spring Lake, probably the prettiest of the shore communities, is just a few miles east of Allaire on Route 524. In this unspoiled turn-of-the-century town, be sure to see the octagonal Portuguese Pavilion (at 207 Atlantic Avenue), the Missouri State Building (411 Ocean Road), the Atlas Home (410 Passaic Avenue), the Osborn Farmhouse dating from 1840 (412 Sussex Avenue), Monmouth House Hotel, Warren Hotel, Essex-Sussex Hotel, the railroad station, and the charming rustic bridges across Spring Lake itself. You might wish to see the sights via trolley, which leaves Monday-Friday from Third and Morris avenues on the hour and half hour, from 10:00 A.M. to 3:30 P.M.. The inexpensive 30-minute ride is picturesque and fun.

Another town to visit, Ocean Grove, a Victorian village founded by Methodists, is described in walk 7.

2
A Shore Path Below the Palisades
Englewood Cliffs

HOW TO GET THERE:

To the Englewood Boat Basin: George Washington Bridge, Palisades Parkway north to exit 1. Bear left after the exit ramp and go down the steep (but wide) road. Follow signs to the Englewood Boat Basin. (From April 1 to November 1 there is a small parking fee.)

Alpine Boat Basin: George Washington Bridge, Palisades Parkway north to exit 2. Follow signs to the Alpine Boat Basin.

The towering, majestic cliffs of the Palisades are among the great natural wonders of our region. Situated on the west bank of the Hudson, directly across from upper Manhattan, the Bronx, and Westchester County, they extend for about 40 miles north along the New Jersey and New York shorelines. These formations were named "palisades" because their impressive rampart-like structure reminded the early settlers of a palisade enclosure. In the 19th century the rock of the Palisades was quarried to such an extent as to threaten their very existence. Fortunately, the Palisades Interstate Park Commission was formed in 1900, just in time to preserve this precious natural wonder. As you drive across the George Washington Bridge and catch your first glimpse of the dramatic and wondrous cliffs, you're thankful they still exist.

The Shore Path below the Palisades is one of two main walks here, the other being the Long Path, on top. Although both provide wonderful river views and great walking, we especially like the Shore Path. You are always close to the river and feel a certain intimacy with your surroundings; there is a wonderful variety in the terrain along the shore (including a long, slender waterfall); and the views of the cliffs are spectacular from below. But what makes this walk so special is your feeling of being in an isolated spot, far from the congestion of the city, when in fact you are so close. As you walk along you hear sounds of the gently lapping water and the wind blowing through the trees, and only an occasional motorboat making its way up or down the river. The Shore Path is pleasantly shaded all the way, with dense woodlands of oaks and maples that turn strikingly brilliant in the fall.

The trail begins near the George Washington Bridge and continues some 10 miles or so north to the New York State line. However, we suggest you concentrate on the section between the Englewood Boat Basin and the Alpine Boat Basin (starting at either place), about five miles in all. If energy level and time are not a problem, you might want to do the entire distance, ideally arranging to be met by car at the other end. If you start at the Alpine Boat Basin you will have to walk only about 1.5 miles before reaching the scenic waterfall, so a walk there and back again might be another option. The going is fairly easy and mostly flat, except for a few stone stairs near the Alpine Boat Basin.

Although the trail is never crowded (you might meet an occasional Boy Scout troop or a solitary walker or two), we suggest you go off-season, rather than during the summer when the parking lots in both basins are noisy and crowded. You might want to take along a pair of binoculars to view the river life (occasional waterfowl and other birds) or the shoreline across the river and the more distant Manhattan skyline.

THE WALK

Park your car at the Englewood Boat Basin, preferably at the northern end of the second of two extensive parking areas, past playgrounds, picnic areas, and fishing docks. In front of you, next to a gigantic boulder at river's edge, is the Shore Path heading north. Although its white markers are somewhat sporadic, it has been well trod and is clearly delineated all the way.

The path's surface, at first sandy, becomes progressively grassy, then somewhat rocky, then woodsy. While the footing is varied—but mostly flat and easy—because of its irregular surface, you are not likely to see bikers or joggers. Truly, this is a peaceful, reflective walk. As you go north, you pass a stretch that was once a settlement of small farms, quarries, and fishing shacks before the parkland was created. You'll see the curious remains of a cem-

SHORE WALK
BELOW
THE
PALISADES

CLOSTER DOCK RD.
ALPINE, N.J
BOAT BASIN
PALISADES INT. PKWY
THE PALISADES SCENIC DRIVING ROAD
WALKING PATH
FALLS
HUDSON RIVER
RTE. 9W
EXIT 1
TO NYC.
TO GEORGE WASHINGTON BRIDGE TO NYC.
PATH TO BRIDGE
ENGLEWOOD BOAT BASIN

N
W E
S

etery, romantically situated amid a pretty meadow. The winding path, always shaded and pleasant, skirts the river, at times so close you can touch the water. You walk past small beaches and docks and rocky lookout points. Trees grow down to the riverbank and honeysuckle and grape vines, tall grasses, and shrubs of wild berries adorn the way. Stone picnic tables assembled from the fallen rock and resembling prehistoric formations are found here and there. After some three miles you reach the picturesque Greenbrook Falls, amid a deeply wooded setting. The path then becomes somewhat steeper (although still easy for most walkers), with occasional stone steps up and down past the washouts on the river's edge. We found this part of the walk particularly appealing, with its variety of vegetation and terrain. After another mile or so (about 5.5 miles from the Englewood Boat Basin) you arrive at the Alpine Boat Basin, where there are more parking areas, fishing docks, picnic tables, a refreshment stand (in season) and rest room facilities.

If you still have energy and want to continue farther north, you will eventually come to the monumental rockfall known as the "Giant Stairs"—actually part of the trail and marked as such with white blazes. This section is somewhat difficult, and recommended only to those who are agile of foot. After some 15 minutes of this strenuous rock climbing, you will regain the regular shore path.

AFTER YOUR WALK

You might enjoy driving north to several Hudson River villages after your walk. We suggest Piermont, about five miles north of Alpine off of Route 9W (turn right at Tallman Park or .5 mile farther at the Piermont sign on your right); or continue on River Road through charming Grand View-on-Hudson on to Nyack, about three miles farther north.

3

Three Mushroom Forays
Cheesequake State Park
Jenny Jump State Forest
Stokes State Forest

HOW TO GET TO THESE THREE LOCATIONS:

Cheesequake State Park: From NY take either Route 80 or New Jersey Turnpike to the Garden State Parkway south. Take exit 120, which is Lawrence Harbor Road. Make 3 right turns: Lawrence Harbor Road, Cliffwood Avenue, and Gordon Road. Gordon Road goes right to the entrance.

Jenny Jump State Forest: Take Route 80 from the George Washington Bridge. Turn off at Route 521 south (exit 12). Drive into Hope and make a left at the light, right on Route 611, and left at Fairview Road to the park.

Stokes State Forest: Take Route 80 from the George Washington Bridge. Turn at Netcong exit onto Route 206 north. This road will take you directly to the parklands.

While mushroom walks have long been popular in Europe, they are a recent U.S. discovery. The New Jersey Mycological Society has some 300 members, and their outings are well attended. Among their favorite spots for hunting mushrooms are Cheesequake State Park, Stokes State Forest, and Jenny Jump State Forest. The society has frequent outings to these three locations, among many others, and we encourage you to call them (see below for information) and to go on a congenial walk with an expert in attendance. While there are more than 30,000 varieties of mushrooms, only several hundred are known edibles. A few dozen are gourmet delights. About two dozen are deadly poisonous, and the society's newsletter often describes terrible errors made by those who do not know one mushroom from another. For this reason, and because the society has all the specifics on what to look for and where, we recommend that you join up with them (either as guest or member) for a mushrooming foray.

The outings of the Mycological Society are listed in advance. You can find out about them by calling Sue or Geoff Kibby in Oldwick, New Jersey, at 201-439-3614, or by writing to them at P.O. Box 291, Oldwick, N.J. 08858. The society is a nonprofit organization that goes on regular forays under experienced leaders on Sunday mornings (starting at 10:00 A.M.), from May to October. Among the delights of a walk with the group are the beautiful locations of these three natural settings, as well as elaborate mushroom-filled meals the society dishes up at various times. Joint trips with other mycological societies are also arranged in surrounding areas and farther afield, including Massachusetts, the Adirondacks, Long Island, and even abroad. Some of these distant outings last for several days. The mushroom forays are held rain or shine, so you should dress accordingly. You should take paper bags (never plastic, which could damage the mushrooms) or waxed paper, a knife, and a basket. Hiking shoes and mosquito repellent are recommended. You should also take a picnic lunch. The leader will explain to you the proper system for cutting, identifying, sorting, and preserving your mushrooms. Collectors are encouraged to bring cameras and/or sketching materials to record their finds. The society will help you with identification charts and other material. Do not bring alcohol or dogs.

We recommend this sort of excursion primarily to adults. Both Stokes and Jenny Jump state parks are quite hilly, so you should be comparatively energetic and surefooted, but the walkers take their time as they hunt. This is not a walk to hurry through! The best season for mushrooming is late summer and fall. The right time and location for the prized morel, for example, is researched by the organization and trips are planned accordingly.

We want to reiterate the advice of the experts: Don't pick and eat any mushroom unless you have the advice of a knowledgeable guide! These are among the few walks that we don't encourage you to do on your own.

AFTER THE WALK

If you enjoy picking your own vegetables—including strawberries, squash, zucchini, and pumpkins—you'll like Matarazzo Farms, not far from Jenny Jump State Forest, on Route 519 near Belvidere. (For information call 201-475-3671.) This is a large produce farm that welcomes you from May to the end of November.

4

An Indoor Garden Walk
Doris Duke Gardens, Somerville

HOW TO GET THERE:

George Washington Bridge to Route 80, to Interstate 287 south, to exit 13 at junction with Route 206 south, to the Somerset Shopping Center. The gardens are located 1.25 miles south of the shopping center, with the entrance on the right. From midtown Manhattan you can take the New Jersey Turnpike to Route 287 north.

During the cold winter months no outing is more cheerful than visiting these splendid interconnected hothouses about an hour from New York. The Duke Gardens are part of the estate of Doris Duke, the tobacco heiress, and are one of New Jersey's major attractions. From the moment you drive through the imposing iron gates with their black eagles on top, you feel as if you had entered a magical world of free-roaming deer, exotic flowers, and mythical trees. The fact that you are picked up at the entrance in a van and transported to this fantasy environment adds to the special ambiance.

The conservatories are surrounded by acres of woodsy parkland, with trees planted in formal rows, reminiscent of a European estate. The greenhouses themselves, built in the late 19th century for family use, are beautiful. Their ornate glass structure is in an Edwardian conservatory style that is carried into several of the indoor gardens.

The full acre of display gardens was opened to the public in 1964. The Duke family maintains strict control over the management of the estate, and there are many regulations to protect the environment and the valuable plants.

Each of the eleven hothouses has a different theme. You walk from one to the next (in the company of a knowledgeable guide and several other visitors) in about one hour's time. These are total landscape environments that follow the traditions of various countries and eras; there are statuary, rock paths, bridges, and pagodas, as well as a profusion of exotic flowers, shrubs, and trees.

This is a walk that we highly recommend for all adults, including the elderly. Although it is not difficult, women are advised to wear flat shoes, as the footing is sometimes awkward over occasional rocky paths. We do not suggest that you bring children, unless they are particularly interested in plants. It is definitely a decorous walk in which everything is rare and special. Cameras are not allowed, nor should you touch anything. There are neither eating or drinking facilities, nor are there picnic grounds.

The gardens are open from October through March, seven afternoons a week, from noon to 4:00 P.M.. On Wednesday and Thursday evenings there are additional tours from 8:30 to 10:30. To visit the gardens you must make advance reservations by calling 201-722-3700. Call about a week ahead of time. There is an entrance fee (currently $5.00). You are not allowed to wander at will, but must accompany a tour (limited to ten people).

THE WALK

Park next to the entrance gate and wait to be picked up by a van, which takes you to the visitors' center. From there your escort takes you to the entrance of the conservatories.

The first stop, the Italian garden, is a wonderful beginning. It includes luxuriant blooms of mimosa, bird-of-paradise, orange and pink bougainvillea, Italian statuary and fountains, gravel paths, and an aura of 19th-century romance.

From there you go to the American Colonial garden, more orderly and classical, with well-groomed hedges, baby's tears ground cover, camellia bushes, huge rounded magnolias, and hanging pink and white petunias. White latticework and brick trimmed paths add to the Colonial flavor.

The next conservatory—the Edwardian garden—is filled with orchids of every size and brilliant color. White, purple, and magenta blossoms are set off by the deep green of rubber plants and palms in the warm, humid surroundings. The orchids are supplied by other greenhouses on the grounds. This is the quintessential garden of turn-of-the-century romantic novels.

The formal French garden is next. Eighteenth-century latticework surrounds this charming formal arrangement of stone paths, niches, ivy-festooned columns, statuary, delicate fountains, and wonderful flowery designs including a giant fleur de lis of brightly colored plants arranged in the style of the gardens of Versailles.

A group of English gardens follows. There is an herb garden, a rockery, a topiary garden, and a marvelous freestyle annual garden with wonderful color combinations.

Next, contrasting with this brilliance, is the desert garden with dirt floor and giant cactuses reaching up to the glass ceiling. The ambiance is that of the American Southwest: brown and gray-green tones in knobby, fantastic shapes, giving the visitor the sense of wild, untamed nature.

We then come to the Chinese garden, an oasis of peace and tranquillity. Not as colorful as the European-style flower gardens, it is nonetheless one of the most appealing. Rock formations and goldfish in small ponds, delicate arching stone bridges, mysterious grottoes for contemplation, leaning willows, and a zigzag walk to ward off evil spirits are among the engaging aspects of this traditional Chinese garden.

The Japanese garden is more stylized, with an elegant teahouse, tiny running streams, miniature wooden bridge, contemplation area with carefully raked soil to represent waves, and the classic gnarled tree forms of Japanese landscape.

An impressive Indo-Persian garden comes next. The most striking feature is its geometric design, from the patterned cutout white walls and long reflecting pool to the crisp designs made by the yellow, orange, and white flowers and citrus trees. Although it represents an Islamic summer palace garden, it seems almost like an illustration to a fairy tale.

The tropical rain forest garden is a mass of jungle plants of many different sizes and shapes of green, with an occasional ladyslipper orchid hidden in the foliage. Spanish moss, banana plants, and huge elephant ears proliferate.

The semitropical garden in the Mediterranean style is the last. Many kinds of purple flowers decorate the edges of the brick paths and terrace, while gloxinias and gardenias in large urns and hanging bougainvillea add brilliant color to the gray-green ferns.

Your own garden might seem very pale after this visit!

AFTER THE WALK

After your walk you might want to drive the 17 miles south to visit Princeton University. See walk 10.

5
Strolling Through a Vineyard
Tewksbury Wine Cellars, Lebanon

HOW TO GET THERE:

From midtown Manhattan: Take the Lincoln Tunnel to New Jersey Turnpike to Route 287 west. Go west on 78 at its intersection with 287. Take exit 24 (Oldwick). Drive past Oldwick on Route 517 for about 3.5 miles. Turn left on Sawmill Road, continue for .5 mile, and bear right at the fork onto Burrell Road. Tewksbury Wine Cellars is about half a mile up the road.
From the George Washington Bridge, take Route 80 west to Route 287 south. Go west on Route 78 and follow directions above.

Strolling through a vineyard—particularly at harvest time—can be very appealing. Because grapes need as much sun as possible, vineyards tend to be located in valleys or hillsides with the maximum sun exposure. They are usually open, airy places in a smiling landscape, and a walk through them can be most pleasant. It is particularly satisfying to go in late summer or early fall—when the mature plants are laden with plump fruit ready to be picked and smelling delicious. It is a time of abundance, when the visitor is especially aware of nature's growing cycle. The grapes will soon be picked and turned into wine. The atmosphere brings to mind ancient rites of harvesting and wine making.

Although it is certainly informative to be guided through a vineyard on a tour and to learn about the elaborate process of wine making, we enjoyed wandering about at will and getting the feel of what it's like. Some vineyard owners—like Tewksbury's—allow this, while others are reluctant to do so. With the burgeoning interest in wines, our region—particularly New Jersey, upstate New York, and Long Island—has become dotted with vineyards, large and small. We found Tewksbury Wine Cellars, in New Jersey's Hunterdon County, ideal for a stroll on a sunny early autumn afternoon.

To get to Tewksbury, you drive through winding roads, past farms and woodlands. Its setting is pastoral, on a picturesque

A Vineyard Walk

TEWKSBURY VINEYARD

BURRELL RD.

SAW MILL RD.

3½ miles

VILLAGE of OLDWICK

W————e

N

S

TO CLINTON

ROUTE 78

523

TO FLEMINGTON

TO NEWARK and RTE. 287 to N.Y.C.

hillside with pleasing views of a rolling landscape. Here you can have a tour of the winery (on weekends) or you can take a stroll on your own at any time. There are wine tastings (you can buy their wines on the premises), and you may even have the opportunity to chat with the resident wine maker. The atmosphere is informal, friendly, and inviting.

In addition to the 20-acre vineyard itself, there is a picturesque 18th-century stone house (where the owner lives) and some old red barns (where the wine is produced). Surrounding them are fields where the owner's horses and cows graze, adding further charm to the place. Down the hill there is a small pond with picnic tables nearby for visitors. While the ideal time of year to visit is early fall or late summer, it can be lovely in spring and summer. There are two annual festivals that might influence when you decide to go: a spring festival (on Father's Day weekend), and a harvest festival (always the third weekend of September). Wintertime brings a stark, surreal beauty to the place, with rows of bare vines and their supports. The winery is open all year (in winter, weather permitting), but we suggest a telephone call—201-832-2400—first to make sure.

Tewksbury Wine Cellars, which prides itself on producing

award-winning wines from European grapes, was founded in 1979 by one Dr. Vernon, a local veterinarian and wine enthusiast who still owns and operates it. About 80 percent of the grapes used in Tewksbury's wine comes from the vineyard; the other 20 percent is imported from California and Europe. The annual production is about 50,000 bottles, which is average for New Jersey wineries but tiny compared to those in California, for example.

Anyone interested in wine or in nature in general would like this walk. Because you can go at your own pace and stay for as long as you like, this is an outing recommended for just about anyone. The short climb up to the vineyard itself is somewhat steep, however, and might be tiring to some less fit walkers.

THE WALK

Park in the parking area to the left of the road, marked with a small wooden sign. Walk to the group of old buildings ahead on your right, where you'll see a sign for the entrance. Walk into a cheery and cozy room where you'll be greeted by a staff member. If you go on a weekend, you might want to take the brief but informative tour that is offered continually, from noon to 5:00 P.M. on Saturdays and Sundays. On this informal tour you are given a concise description of the various stages of wine making— the harvesting, the pressing of the grapes, the fermentation, aging, and bottling and corking—all of which takes place in two smallish rooms. You are shown the huge stainless steel vats and sweet-smelling oak barrels that are used in the process. After this ten-or-so minute tour, you might want to taste some wine. For a small fee (which is reimbursed in case you decide to buy some bottles), you are given samplings of Riesling, Gewürtztraminer, Seyval Blanc, Chambourcin, or apple wine, to name a few. You should now feel reinforced and ready for your vineyard stroll.

Walk past the old stone house, where you'll see a dirt road to the left going up a gentle slope. Take that path, which leads (after less than .25 of a mile) to the bottom of the vineyard. Rows and rows of vines are nestled on this hillside, surrounded by views of rolling hills and forests. Unless you are a connoisseur of grapes and care to locate specific plants, we suggest you walk randomly on the mowed grass paths that separate the rows of vines to get a feel of this special environment. You can meander about as you wish, up, down, around, cutting through here and there, making this walk as short or as long as you like. As you walk along amid the vines, you'll feel a sense of peace and quiet interrupted only by the occasional songs of birds . . . and a mechanical song designed to keep the real birds at bay. We saw grasshoppers and white butterflies fluttering about the plants, and smelled the subtle odor of grapes that permeates the air. The bunches of the plentiful fruit are in delicate shades of purple, mauve, and various intensities of green, and look as though they had been painted in a still life. Although this is not a "pick-your-own" outing, you might see members of the vineyard's staff out there during harvest time. Observing the picking process makes you realize how long and laborious a job it is (and how basically unchanged it is from ancient times).

AFTER THE WALK

Drive back down the hill to the tiny village of Oldwick (which you passed on your way to the winery), one long block of vintage Victorian houses and picturesque 18th-century buildings. Founded in the 1740s as "New Germantown" by German immigrants, Oldwick was built around the Zion Evangelical Lutheran Church, New Jersey's oldest Lutheran congregation. This historic church (refurbished in the 19th century) houses some precious village documents, as well as the impressive royal charter granted by George III in 1767. (The church is always open; its large black iron key is purported to hang in a local kitchen.) Surrounding the church is a quaint old cemetery filled with 18th- and 19th-century graves. Some of the markers have well-preserved carvings and easily distinguishable lettering. Another attractive church, the Oldwick Methodist Church, is a tall, white, stately Victorian structure with rounded windows. And the general store, dating from 1760, is fun to browse through; there is a small restaurant in back. For a fancier lunch or dinner, try the Tewksbury Inn, another building of the early 1800s. You can also visit antique shops that line the street, as well as the delightful Trailtree Book Shop.

6

A Short Brookside Walk in the Woods
Jones Road Park, Englewood

HOW TO GET THERE:

George Washington Bridge to Route 4; take first exit (Jones Road). Go north (right turn) on Jones Road for several blocks. Park is on your right.

Once the wooded property of a private estate, this unusually nice hillside has a brook, its own waterfall, and a pond at the top. The path, beginning with a picnic and playing area, soon becomes surprisingly away-from-it-all, considering that you are only three or four blocks from the roar of the highway you came on. The trail, nicely marked with white blazes, is slightly hilly at all times, but the going is easy and the brook with its big boulders is always right beside you. For a pleasantly uncrowded woodland site literally only five minutes from the George Washington Bridge, you can't do better, unless you want a more extended walk. This is not a long hike, perhaps half an hour at most.

There is a large, flat, grassy play area below the woodland climb, where you can cook out or play Frisbee or watch the ducks on the stream. An ideal place to take children, this park is popular with young people from the neighborhood, but they do not seem to leave the flat area for the hilly climb. However, kids love the path up with the shallow running brook, which is fun to climb over (or fall into, as one of ours did once). At the top you'll see the mansion to which this parkland formerly belonged, as well as the pond that supplies the ever-running waterfall and stream.

You might want to bring a picnic or the makings of a cookout and make a day of it, as there are tables and grills. (There are also many refreshment spots in nearby Englewood.) You can enjoy this walk at any time of year; of course, it is deserted in late fall and winter.

THE WALK

Leave your car right on Jones Road, parked as near as possible to the fence. Walk directly across the park, following the brook toward the woods. The trail has a white blaze at the entrance just to the right of the stream. The footing is mostly pine needles and mulch, and is pleasant going. There are one or two step-ups, but nothing difficult. At the top you'll find a great flat boulder for sitting and contemplating the waterfall and pond. You can continue at the top for a short distance around the pond, but soon you realize that houses are not far away. An ideal outing for families with young children who would find a longer walk tiring, this one offers a nice combination of playground, brook, forest, and stream.

AFTER THE WALK

You might want to combine this visit with another nearby park outing: Fort Lee Historic Park. This park, set right atop the Palisades just south of the George Washington Bridge, is the site of a Revolutionary fort, and it contains a reconstructed series of structures, military defenses, and even a little cabin where sometimes you'll find a few people dressed as Revolutionary War characters roasting a leg of lamb on a spit. Recently a reenactment of a battle was held in very realistic terms at this park. But even if you come on an average day, it's a nice place to view the Hudson, and the historic scenes and setups are interesting and quite well done. To get there from Jones Road Park, go back to Route 4 toward the George Washington Bridge, taking the last Fort Lee exit, which will bring you to Main Street. The park is at the very easternmost end of Main Street, at Hudson Terrace, as, of course, it fronts on the river cliffs. There is a small charge in season for parking.

7

A Walk Through a Methodist Village on the Shore
Ocean Grove

HOW TO GET THERE:

From midtown Manhattan take the New Jersey Turnpike south to exit 11 onto the Garden State Parkway south. Take exit 100B and Route 33 east. Follow signs to Ocean Grove.
From George Washington Bridge take Route 80 to the Garden State Parkway and follow same directions as above.

The village of Ocean Grove is a one-of-a-kind shore community. When you think of taking a walk in most shore towns near New York City, you usually find busy, commercial places with little charm. Not so with Ocean Grove. Located on the New Jersey shore one hour's drive south of the city, it contrasts sharply with its neighbors. This is a picturesque town of delightful Victorian gingerbread houses, small hotels, and tiny shops lining pleasantly shaded streets. A fine, wide promenade runs along the oceanfront. Of note is a giant architectural wonder—the Great Auditorium— and dozens of little painted structures for camp meetings.

Ocean Grove's location is what appealed to its founders, a group of Methodist ministers and lay people who, in 1869, came from Philadelphia to conduct a revival meeting. They pitched their tents in this quiet ocean retreat, creating a religious seaside resort in which to pursue annual summer meetings in relative isolation. Facing the ocean and flanked on both sides by two small lakes (Wesley Lake and Fletcher Lake), they thought the area was "removed from the dissipations and follies of fashionable water places." By 1874 the tent community—known as "little canvas village"—included about 200 ministers during the height of the season and almost 700 tents with permanent floors and small kitchens for the community. The Methodist Camp Meeting Association, which ran the community, remained a private association, so that it could maintain strict control over the inhabitants of the resort. Lots were leased for 99 years, with the option to renew! Strict regulations included no alcohol, smoking, organ grinders, peddlers, vendors, or carriages on the beach; no swearing in boats on Lake Wesley, no newspapers on Sunday, no dancing, and no card playing. The gates of the resort closed daily at 10:00 P.M. and remained closed all day on Sunday. In fact, no one could do much of anything on Sunday—except attend religious meetings. Trains were not allowed to stop at the Ocean Grove/Asbury Park station (much to the annoyance of the inhabitants of Asbury Park), and no one could enter the community on Sunday except on foot (over the footbridges of Wesley Lake). Indeed,

President Ulysses S. Grant, who once visited his mother and sister on a Sunday at their rented Ocean Grove Cottage, was obliged to walk into town, like anyone else. His carriage waited for him outside the town gates.

There *were* a few recreational outlets for visitors to Ocean Grove, however. They were allowed to stroll on the boardwalk and go boating on Wesley Lake. For some time the town fathers thought of banning swimming altogether (because of the inevitable disrobing it entailed), but they agreed to it, reluctantly, with some conditions. (Of course, swimming was forbidden on Sundays.)

Most of the life of Ocean Grove centered around the auditorium (which you can still visit), an immense and curious edifice built in 1894 to accommodate 10,000 people and a 500-person choir. (It was constructed without nails in imitation of Solomon's temple in the Bible.) Here, during camp meetings, religious services were held daily, on a continuous basis. Ocean Grove still holds religious and musical programs in this auditorium; indeed, the town remains a religious retreat for many, who still set up tents in summer. Although its blue laws have disappeared, it maintains a pristine and pure quality, which adds to its charm. (It was this special ambiance that appealed to Woody Allen, when he chose it as the location for his film *Stardust Memories* some years ago.)

We think that walking through this unspoiled town, with its wonderful boardwalk and refreshing ocean breezes, makes for a pleasant outing for just about anyone, young or old. The atmosphere is relaxed and casual, conducive to a leisurely stroll. Unless people-watching is your favorite sport, we recommend a visit to Ocean Grove off-season, for even here there is inevitably more congestion and activity during the summer months. (And driving to and from the Jersey Shore in summer can be a nightmare.)

THE WALK

Park your car wherever you can, preferably along Main Avenue, in the center of town. We recommend you pick up a walking map, available at one of the realtors (or other shops) on the street. On Main Avenue you'll find many small shops and an array of Victorian houses with gingerbread porches, painted in the most original color combinations. Walk toward the ocean for your stroll along the uncluttered boardwalk. You'll see a fishing pier and two wide and well-maintained bathing beaches. After you have filled your lungs with the clean ocean air, you can begin your exploration of the rest of the town. Don't miss Ocean Pathway, a picture-postcard street lined with trees and park benches. You can understand why this street is often photographed: rarely do you have the opportunity to see such a collection of charming and unusual Victorian houses. Make a detour or two to discover some of the other quaint streets that run parallel to Ocean Pathway, starting at Ocean Avenue. Of course the part of town that is of particular interest is the religious complex, including the Great Auditorium, the Tabernacle, the Founders Park, Thornley Chapel, and the remains of some of the tents. You can reach these surprisingly offbeat buildings by walking on Pilgrim Pathway, Central Avenue, or their cross streets. There are squares, pleasant parks, and curious little streets to see at every turn, and you can meander about as long as you like. Finally, you might enjoy walking across Wesley Lake (toward Asbury Park) on the same bridges that were used by many a Sunday walker 100 years ago. You'll notice a sharp contrast between the well-preserved Ocean Grove and its nearby urban neighbor.

AFTER THE WALK

After your walk you might enjoy a visit to Allaire Village (see walk 1) or to Spring Lake, another pleasant waterfront village, about 15 minutes south of Ocean Grove.

8
Total Fitness Trail
Shark River County Park, Monmouth County

HOW TO GET THERE:

From midtown Manhattan, take the New Jersey Turnpike south to exit 11 onto the Garden State Parkway South.
From George Washington Bridge take Route 80 to the Garden State Parkway. Take exit 100B onto Route 33 east for a few minutes. Turn right at Schoolhouse Road and follow signs for Shark River County Park, which will be on your right.

You may think you are a fit walker, but you haven't tried anything until you've completed the Fitness Trail at Shark River County Park. Unlike steep climbs that test only your hiking endurance, this trail is a real workout for the total physical fitness buff. We hasten to add that this is also a very pretty walk, even if you just amble through and ignore the fearsome instructions you'll find at every turn.

The trail combines jogging, exercising, and a balanced program of total fitness along a trail of about 1.5 miles. There are 32 exercise stations, each with instructions, a course marker, and apparatus where necessary. You can monitor your heartbeat at regular intervals, following the instructions provided. There are both competitive and less competitive levels. The trail stresses flexibility (for greater coordination in sports), muscle tone (to strengthen and build up your muscles), and cardiovascular conditioning.

Meanwhile, you are walking (or running) on a fairly flat, sandy trail, with scrub pines and dune vegetation typical of the Atlantic shoreline. This pleasant walk is nice in any season and is usually quite deserted, for obvious reasons. (We did see one poor soul emerging from the trail with a sprained ankle.) Following is more about the struggles that await anyone brave enough to attempt a full-scale assault on the trail.

Obviously, if you intend to follow the instructions, you should be in excellent physical shape. Of course, you can pick and choose which exercises you wish to do and can walk instead of run from one station to the next. Children with good energy will love the challenges of this outing and will never be bored. Be sure to wear your running shoes (if you're going to run) and comfortable exercise clothes; and take along a stopwatch if you are a competitive athletic type. There are picnic grounds and regular nature trails across the road (in the same park), so you can bring your own refreshments The park is open from 8:00 A.M. until dusk, year-round.

THE WALK

Park your car in the lot and cross the road away from the picnic area. There are signs indicating where the fitness trail begins and explaining its use. At first you will see only an ordinary woodsy path, but soon exercise no. 1 appears. After you have completed your first stretches numerous times (they tell you how many of everything to do) you are horrified to realize there are 31 more such activities planned for you! Among them are leg bends, push-ups, step-ups, a vault, balance beam, stretches, jumps, back exercises, monkey bars, and breathing exercises. You are expected to run or jog from station to station. Periodically you test your heartbeat, understanding that you should stop exercising if you do not meet the recommendations. The apparatus used for the exercises is discreetly unobtrusive; made of weathered wood, it sits in woodsy alcoves to the side of the trail. The path makes a circle, bringing you back to the same place from which you started when you were young and fresh—and less fit!

AFTER THE WALK

After your walk, visit the two Jersey shore villages of Ocean Grove and Spring Lake (see walk 7). These are two of the nicest and least spoiled communities on this northern part of the coast, and both have wonderful ocean beaches for walking or swimming, although some areas of the beach are restricted to residents.

9

Walking Through a Moravian Village
Hope

From the George Washington Bridge, take Route 80 west, exit at Route 521 south (exit 12) and go for a couple of miles until you come to Hope.

It comes as a surprise to many who are only familiar with urban and suburban New Jersey that a good part of the state is rural, with rolling hills and farmlands. As you drive through these areas, you occasionally come across some quaint little towns and villages that have their own particular charm. Hope is among these picturesque villages.

The town, with its Moravian heritage, has an especially intriguing history. The Moravians—a pious, hardworking religious sect from Moravia and Bohemia (now Czechoslovakia)—came to the United States beginning in 1735 to escape persecution. In 1768 one Samuel Green offered a group of Moravians 1,000 acres of land on which to build a settlement. They paid 1,000 pounds sterling.

The community developed fully by about 1774, when a plan was drawn up by the bishop of the mother church in Europe; Hope was one of the first planned communities in this country. (The town plan remains virtually intact today.)

The large stone grist mill at the bottom of High Street was one of the town's earliest structures. The limestone Gemeinhaus (corner of Union and High streets), built a few years later, was at first a community center and place of worship, later a courthouse, and finally a bank.

During the Revolutionary War the Moravians, like the Quakers, were conscientious objectors and refused to fight. However, they provided excellent nursing care for the wounded.

Unfortunately, the settlement of Hope did not last long. By 1791 a serious decline began, and by 1799 the population had been reduced from 147 to only 84. In 1807, after a severe smallpox epidemic, the Moravians decided to sell their community for $48,000. The remaining Moravians moved to Bethlehem, Pennsylvania. Before their departure, they performed a final service of worship in the Gemeinhaus and at the cemetery on Easter Sunday, April 17, 1808.

This village of stone buildings has remained much the same to this day, and you will enjoy its unusual flavor as you walk the narrow streets. As of our last visit there was no place to eat or drink in or near the village. We suggest that you bring your own picnic or eat before or afterward at the Martha Washington Pub in nearby Blairstown. You might want to pick up a simple guide to the town, available at several shops, or use the numbered tour guide outlined below. Although an easy walk, Hope is not recommended for children unless they are interested in history and architecture. It's a quiet town with few distractions. There is a quaint cemetery where you can make grave rubbings of the early markers.

Autumn is lovely here. The hillsides and surroundings of Hope are spectacular if you catch them at the right time. You will find maples (including the striped maple), pines, various kinds of birch, elms, beech, aspens, and hemlocks in the vicinity, and in the fall—and spring—the landscape is glorious. Birds love this tree-filled region.

THE WALK

As you walk around Hope, note some of the features typical of Moravian architecture: the economical use of cut stone (used only in cornerstones or quoins and around doors and windows); red brick window arches and chimneys; some limestone window arches; and, in some cases, two-story attics that make for balanced design proportions.

A walking tour of Hope should start at the Grist Mill, at the foot of High Street. (Numbers are keyed to map.)

1. Grist Mill (1769–1770). Oldest building in the village. During the Revolutionary War it was used to grind grain for Washington's troops.

2. Moravian distillery (1775). Rye whiskey and beer were produced (on the ground floor). The brewmaster and his family occupied the second floor. Unfortunately, only a part of the building is still in existence.

3. Farmhouse and barn (1775–1776). Oldest remaining residence.

4. Peter Worbass, the first settler in Hope, built a log cabin in 1769 on this site. The cellar of the existing house might have been part of his cabin.

5. Site of the Moravian log tavern (1773). George Washington visited in 1782. A church was later (1841) built on this site; the present building was destroyed by fire in 1918 and restored in the 1950s as a community center.

6. Moravian long house (1771). One of the earliest stores occupied this site.

7. Moravian store and residence (1776). Built by Frederick Leinbach, Peter Worbass's successor as town manager, when it seemed that Hope would be a thriving community.

8. House (1787).

9. House (1785).

10. House (1775). The second house built by the community. Later, in 1807, it was used as the schoolhouse.

11. House (1774–1776).

12. Moravian Cemetery. Contains 62 graves, all very simple and plain. On each slab you can read the name, birth, and death date and a number that corresponds to the list of burials in the Moravian Archives at Bethlehem, Pennsylvania.

13. Site of St. John's United Methodist Church (1832). The present building dates from 1879.

14. St. Luke's Episcopal Church (1832). Built of native limestone. Note the interior spiral staircase, supposedly copied from a design by Sir Christopher Wren.

15. Gemeinhaus (1781). The place of worship for the community. There were separate staircases for men and women that led to the actual church room on the second floor. The first floor included the living quarters of the pastor and a small school for boys.

16–18. Moravian houses (all dating from 1776).

19. The Moravian school building, also known as the Single Sisters Choir, was the last structure built by the Moravians in Hope (1803). It housed the colony's unmarried women and was also, for a short time, used as a school for boys.

20. Stone Bridge (1807). Not built by the Moravians, although it has been called the Moravian Bridge.

21. Hope Historical Society Museum. Once the bridge toll-house, the museum is open on weekends during the summer.

AFTER THE WALK

If you're an adventurous sort, try gliding and hot air ballooning at Tock's Island Soaring, Inc., on Route 94 just west of Blairstown, which offers rides, rentals, and lessons.

Beachers, rowers, and picnickers should enjoy Mt. Lake Beach in season. It's a small, pretty lakeside area nestled into the surrounding hills. You can rent rowboats, enjoy the pleasant beach (nice for children), and have a picnic here. Take Union Street from Hope, make a left on Lake Justit Road to its end, turn right to Mt. Lake Beach.

There is apple picking in the fall at Race Farm near Blairstown.

10

A University Stroll
Princeton

HOW TO GET THERE:

New Jersey Turnpike to exit 9. Take Route 1 south, then Route 571 west to Princeton. Follow signs for the university.

Princeton University is not just the prettiest school in our area, it's often called one of the most beautiful in the country. The spacious elegance of the campus with its great Gothic buildings and archways, geometric pathways, fine modern buildings, grand trees, charming gardens, outdoor sculpture and lake, and its sense of the gracious past are all easily available to a visiting stroller. The campus provides the walker with acres and acres to wander through, and the town of Princeton itself includes many wonderful areas. You will have to choose your route by how much time you have, for you could spend several days exploring the many areas here.

The University was founded in 1754; Nassau Hall, at its center, was completed two years later and is still in use. Despite bombardment during the Revolution and two fires, the Continental Congress was able to meet there in 1783, when Princeton served as the nation's capital for four months. The school soon began to add buildings and today is a legendary educational institution. There are a fine Gothic chapel (which you should not miss on your walk); the modern Woodrow Wilson School building designed by Minoru Yamasaki; Maclean House, the home of the university's presidents from 1756 to 1879 and now alumni headquarters; Alexander Hall, a Victorian auditorium; the twin Whig and Clio debating society Greek Revival buildings; the fine art museum; and dozens of other interesting sites. You can walk across the spacious lawns from one to another, observing students as they hurry to class or activity, or read in the shadow of the famous Gothic towers or beside a contemporary sculpture. This traditional university is quintessentially "collegiate" and we guarantee you'll enjoy it.

Princeton, the town, faces the campus across the main street, Nassau Street. Shops and restaurants and a bustling atmosphere contrast with the quiet of the campus; you will enjoy visiting Palmer Square in the center of town, as well as several non-university sites. In addition, two other places outside the campus itself are worth seeing: the Grover Cleveland Tower and Graduate College with its fine view, and the Institute for Advanced Study, where Albert Einstein and other great thinkers have worked.

The walk suggested below is only one of many possibilities. The university provides guided tours, if you prefer. If not, we advise you to pick up a full campus map (available at Maclean House) and try to follow the route given below. Alternatively, you can leave your car and just wander about the university, noting whichever buildings you happen to pass and perhaps ending your jaunt by Lake Carnegie at the university boathouse where (in season) you'll see sculls filled with rowers setting off in the swift current.

Any time of year is the right time for this walk. In summer, of course, school is not in session, and you'll miss the full student aura, but the buildings and flowers and shaded walks are all there. (Avoid the major graduation and reunion week in early June and arrival time in mid-September, when parking is impossible.) There are innumerable university events throughout the year, from professional music and theater to sporting events and performances. You might want to coordinate your visit with such an event. The major football games in the fall come complete with band marching across the campus, tiger mascots, and singing groups performing under hallowed arches. Full information and tickets for such events can be obtained by calling 609-452-3000.

Princeton is an almost completely flat area, and therefore walking is not tiring, but the distances are quite large. The paths are generally gravel. Families will enjoy this outing, including older children in particular, who might like to imagine themselves as students someday. You need not bring anything special. Every kind of eatery can be found across the street, and you can pick up all sorts of information and maps on the history, courses, and events at the admissions office at 110 West College.

THE WALK

We suggest that you leave your car outside the campus either at a meter on Nassau Street or at a lot just behind it. Our walk assumes that you are starting off in the center of town at Palmer Square, and entering the gate of the university directly opposite the kiosk. (Numbers are keyed to map.)

1. Maclean House will be the first building on your left. Here you can get an escorted tour of the campus, or a sculpture tour, or just a map to make the tour yourself. For tour reservations, call 609-452-3603. (You can also wait for a tour without reservation.) Maclean House is itself of interest; it once housed Aaron Burr, as well as university presidents from 1756 to 1879.

2. Princeton University's landmark Nassau Hall will be your next stop. Here, beginning in 1756, American history was made.

The Continental Congress worked here when it served as capital of the country. Washington's capture of the building in 1777 ended the Battle of Princeton, and he returned to the hall again in 1783 to receive the thanks of the Congress for his conduct of the war. For some 50 years Nassau Hall contained all of Princeton's classrooms and dormitories, as well as its library, dining room, chapel, and kitchen.

Behind Nassau Hall is Cannon Green, the quadrangle that is the site of the Big Cannon and now the center of many festivities at the college.

3. East Pyne, the building that houses the student center, is next on your tour. Be sure to go inside and see the rotunda.

4. When you come out of East Pyne, you will see Firestone Library, which houses more than 3.5 million books. One of the world's great university libraries, Firestone is worth entering: It has many special collections and is a fascinating place to visit.

5. A stop at the university chapel is not to be missed. Built between 1925 and 1928, it is the third largest college chapel in the world. Its Gothic architecture, inspired by the chapel of King's College, Cambridge, England, is enhanced by exquisite stained-glass windows by American artists. It seats some 2,000 people and is frequently the scene of Princeton weddings.

6. From the chapel, walk through McCosh Hall archway and out into Prospect Avenue, where the mansions housing the university "eating clubs" for upperclassmen and -women are located.

7. At the corner of Prospect and Washington Road you'll find the Woodrow Wilson School, a contemporary and striking building with a reflecting pool. Designed by Minoru Yamasaki, the building opened in 1960 as the home of the School of Economics, Politics, and History. Several notable sculptures are on display here.

8. Turn back toward the School of Architecture, completed in 1963 and housing an architectural laboratory, as well as gallery and studios.

9. Prospect House and Garden are an especially handsome part of the campus. For many years the home of university presidents, this fine mansion was built in 1849 and has had an illustrious history. It now houses dining and social facilities of the university's

faculty and staff, and has attractive, well-tended gardens.

10. The University Art Museum, which is easily recognized by the giant Picasso sculpture in front, is a first-class museum. It is open to the public and includes a notable collection of antiquities, Renaissance paintings, and modern works. It is used by art and art history students, as well as by scholars from around the world.

11 and 12. These twin buildings in the Greek Revival style are across Cannon Green from Nassau Hall. The halls, called Whig and Clio, originally housed the American Whig Society and the Cliosophic Society, the nation's oldest college debating and literary clubs. Extracurricular life revolved around the societies in the 19th century, and a number of notable future politicians debated in them. Today they are still the scene of debates and lectures.

13. West College, constructed in traditional design as a dormitory complex, is typical of the campus style; it is now home to university offices, including the admissions office (where you can pick up a variety of brochures and guidebooks).

14. Alexander Hall with its Richardson Auditorium is an architectural oddity and campus landmark. It was the first building erected by the Presbyterian church in the U.S. for seminary purposes. Its rounded walls and unusual architecture make it well worth visiting, and you will often find an interesting event going on within.

15. Holder Hall is a typical residential building and is part of Rockefeller College. Walk into the quad and you'll get a sense of what living in the university undergraduate area is like. The cloistered walkways and arches are open to wander through, and you're apt to think, *this* is what colleges are supposed to look like!

Cross through the arch back out into Nassau Street and to your parking meter, but don't go home yet. Other campus sites worth visiting are Princeton Inn College, Palmer Stadium, and the boathouse.

In the neighborhood are a number of "don't miss" sites: the Institute for Advanced Study, the Theological Seminary, the Graduate College, and the homes of Thomas Mann, Woodrow Wilson, Albert Einstein, and Paul Robeson. A map obtainable at Maclean

House will direct you to these locations. It also lists a number of old houses in the township and the Princeton Cemetery, where the earliest stones date from 1760.

Finally, you might want to see Morven, a national landmark built by Richard Stockton, a signer of the Declaration of Independence. It is the official residence of the governors of New Jersey and has hosted nine presidents and a variety of kings, queens, and other luminaries.

11

A Fragrance and Sensory Garden Walk
(Especially, but not only, for the blind and handicapped)
Colonial Park, Somerset County

HOW TO GET THERE:

From the George Washington Bridge take Route 80 west onto Route 287 south. After passing Bound Brook take country route 527 (Easton Ave.). Go right on Cedar Grove Lane. Go right again on Weston Road to Elizabeth Avenue. Entrance to park is on your left on Elizabeth Avenue.

From midtown Manhattan take the Lincoln Tunnel to the New Jersey Turnpike, to Route 287 and follow same directions as above.

This extraordinary pair of gardens—one all roses, the other a fragrance and sensory garden—is something special. While it forms only a small one-acre part of a large and spacious county park in Franklin Township, it has a rare quality all its own. Once part of a private estate, the gardens were developed by a horticulturalist when they became part of the public park.

The more unusual of the two gardens is the fragrance and sensory garden. Newly designed with Braille plaques and a low handrail, this garden includes especially interesting flowers and plants to smell and touch. Each example has an unusual quality, such as the soft fuzzy lamb's ears, the fragrant lavender plant, and the tasty mint. As you make your way around the garden, you can feel and smell and even taste these odd, fragrant plants and guess what they are, or read the small plaques. There are soft, spongy plants, prickly plants, and aromatic lemony plants. The flat walkway is made to accommodate the handicapped and visually impaired, with flagstone paving and intersecting strips of brick to indicate changes in direction. There are many charming arbored benches for resting. We also recommend this walk for families with children, as it is quite short.

Adjoining the Sensory and Fragrance Garden is the Rose Garden, and what a rose garden it is! Described as "an encyclopedia of roses," the collection includes 4,000 rosebushes (275 varieties) that bloom from early June all the way into fall. One of the sections is called Grandmother's Garden, which contains old hybrid perpetual and hybrid tea roses, some of which date back to the 1820s. Another part has climbing roses, while the Dutch Garden is in the style of a formal rose garden in Holland. It is a beautifully designed garden that is constantly in bloom during the long season. Everything is identified. A walk through it on the flagstone walks can be broken with little rests on arbored benches. For the rose fancier this is a blissful stroll.

If you are of a romantic disposition, you'll find that both gardens have a touch of another time and place about them. We did—on a hot summer day, with the various flowery aromas wafting through the air, and the cool shaded benches inviting us to rest for a moment.

Colonial Park is a vast park, rather overdeveloped, with something for everyone seeking recreation, from paddle boats to a small foresty nature walk, a nice lilac garden, picnic tables, tennis courts, and a playground, in addition to the gardens described above. There are other walks in the park, of course, including a stroll through the arboretum. Guided tours are also available.

The hours are daily from 10:00 A.M. to 8:00 P.M., from June 1 to November 1.

LONG ISLAND

12

Through the Meadows to the Beach
Caumsett State Park

HOW TO GET THERE:
From uptown Manhattan: Take Cross Bronx Expressway to Throgs Neck Bridge, to Cross Island Parkway, to Long Island Expressway (Route 495), east to Route 110 (exit 49N), north to Route 25A, west to West Neck Road, to Lloyd Harbor Road, to park entrance. From midtown Manhattan: Midtown Tunnel to Long Island Expressway and follow same directions as above.

Caumsett State Park offers an unusually unspoiled and uncrowded walking area through meadows of wildflowers and deep woods to a pristine North Shore beach.

This is a walk for all seasons. In springtime there are masses of buttercups and other wildflowers amid a romantic Constable-like landscape; in summer, the possibility of a great swim; in fall, the vivid colors of foliage; and in winter, wonderful cross-country skiing.

The great advantage of this walk is its unstructured setup: no lifeguards, no snack bars, no facilities—including no way to shorten the walk back. No motorized vehicles (except by special permit) are allowed. The beach is clean and somewhat pebbly, and surrounded with real sand dunes. Fishermen are often the only visitors here.

This 1,475-acre park was once the estate of Marshall Field III, the grandson of the founder of the department store. Field, an imaginative philanthropist whose interests also included civic and educational pursuits as well as the outdoor life, built this estate in the 1920s as a sort of self-sufficient rural community—with its own water and electrical supply and its own dairy and vegetable farm. Converted to a state park in recent years, Caumsett is an especially serene place for a day away.

Located on a beautiful peninsula stretching into Long Island Sound, the park is essentially flat (elevations rise to only 120 feet above sea level). It includes a freshwater pond, marshes (which account for the rich bird life), and many dirt and stony paths crisscrossing to the sea. The beach has some great boulders in addition to a fairly pebbly surface. This is not a fine-sand beach.

While all seasons are recommended for this outing, Caumsett is of course more crowded in summer. But even on weekends the park is not too busy, and on most weekdays it is positively deserted. On a day that we were there we met—in the entire day—only one couple fishing and one artist.

This is not a walk with dramatic cliffs and vistas. The mostly level terrain is good for conversation, nature-watching, and other quiet activities. Its length (about two miles each way, plus one mile along the beach) is not excessive, but the return trip might be hard on small children, because of the lack of public facilities (this, of course, is one of the things that keeps the beach quite empty). We suggest you pick up a map and brochure at the parking booth. Cross-country skiers may also take advantage of the trails and bridle paths through the woods, adding variety to their trek. If you are interested in organized walking tours, Caumsett provides them, too ($1.00 per person, from Labor Day to Memorial Day). Bring water! There are no public concessions, so be sure to take food and beverages (nonalcoholic). Take a bathing suit in summer and plan to change behind some bushes. If you're a birder, take binoculars. As for shoes, we recommend good walking shoes or sneakers for dirt paths, pebbly shoreline, and rocky coastline. While this is not a rigorous walk, the terrain would be hard on bare feet or flimsy shoes. If you like surf fishing, this is the spot, but you need a permit to drive in (though not to fish). If you prefer to bike or jog, you can save your energy for exploring the beach. You will find this area pleasant, although the surface is not ideal. Do *not* bring pets.

The park is open from 8:00 A.M. to 4:30 P.M. daily; there is a small parking fee in season. For information call 516-423-1770.

THE WALK

Park at the lot next to the booth. Set out across the meadow about .3 of a mile, bearing left to pick up a sandy trail (or stay in the

SALT MARSH

LONG ISLAND SOUND

BEACH

CAUMSETT STATE PARK

— LLOYD NECK —

TARGET ROCK WILDLIFE REFUGE

PARK ENTRANCE

LLOYD MANOR HOUSE

LLOYD HARBOR ROAD

LLOYD HARBOR

BLACK OAK TREE

WEST NECK BEACH

HUNTINGTON HARBOR

BIKE PATH

WEST NECK ROAD

LLOYD HARBOR
CAUMSETT STATE PARK
WEST NECK BEACH
TARGET ROCK WILDLIFE REFUGE

↑ TO

N
W
S
E

SNAKE HILL RD.

SHORE RD.

COLD SPRING HARBOR

COLD SPRING BEACH

HARBOR RD.

METHODIST MEETING HOUSE

WHALING MUSEUM

SPRING

MAIN STREET

25A

TO HUNTINGTON

HISTORIC DISTRICT

VALENTINE-DENTON HOUSE

TURKEY LANE

TO GOOSE HILL RD.

VILLAGE of COLD SPRING HARBOR

TO 25A RTE.

STATE FISH HATCHERY

OLD MILL DAM

LAWRENCE HILL RD.

ST. JOHN'S CHURCH

meadows, if you prefer). The trail is wide enough to spot easily. As you can see from the official Caumsett Park map, you have many choices of trails to get to the water. If you choose the most direct route you will go through fields and woods for about a mile and a half, through dense vine-covered forest and past the marsh on the left. You will have gone almost two miles from the start. On the beach, if you bear left, you will come to a point and a cove—about a half mile. For a longer beach walk, turn right and walk for about one mile to some small steps up to a bluff and a return trail. On the beach enjoy sea gulls and wonderful sunbathing rocks where you can stretch out, surrounded by gentle lapping water.

Birders will find an abundance of species in the salt marsh: black crown night herons, green herons, egrets, great blue herons, great white herons, ospreys, gulls, red-winged blackbirds, king-fishers, black ducks, marsh hawks, as well as sparrows. Nature lovers will enjoy the variety of trees, birds, wildflowers, and shells and colorful stones (great skipping stones) on the beach. Plants in and around the marsh include the endangered prickly pear cactus (which you should not touch!), high-water bush, beach plums, sea rocket, as well as the more common goldenrod and dandelions.

While there are no formal picnic sites, we recommend (in addition to large beach rocks, where it might be fun to eat with your feet dangling in the water) that you try the charming grassy shaded lookout area atop the bluffs at the far end of the beach, where the path starts home. Walk home via the freshwater pond and Marshall Field House, despite a fairly steep but mercifully short hill. There are several return routes to choose from; consult your map.

AFTER THE WALK

This is a great area for sight-seeing. In the immediate vicinity, at the end of Lloyd Harbor Road, don't miss the famous 100-foot-tall black oak tree, which is supposed to be the largest of its kind in the country.

Also of interest is the Lloyd Manor House, a white colonial

building which is open to the public and is also situated nearby on Lloyd Harbor Road.

You might enjoy a visit to the nearby village of Cold Spring Harbor. Its importance as a whaling port in the last century has left it a legacy of frame buildings on narrow Main Street, surrounded by waterfront country lanes, and the marshes typical of this part of Long Island. Its charm lies both in its situation on the water and the bustling center of the village that, despite some trendy boutiques, retains the original scale and architecture of the whaling era.

Try a walking tour of about three blocks of Main Street with its charming houses of the early and mid-nineteenth century. Don't miss the Methodist Meeting House, built in 1842, to give the village residents their own church; the Conklin house, at 75 Main Street, built in 1720 and the oldest house in town; Manuel Enos's imposing home, at 208 Main Street; and, among many others, the Valentine-Denton house, at 60 Main Street, which was occupied by whaling captains through the years. The Whaling Museum, also on Main Street, is worth a visit. There you will find a completely outfitted whaling boat that will delight children and nostalgics.

Beyond Main Street, on Route 25A near the junction to Route 108, is the Cold Spring Harbor Fish Hatchery and Aquarium, which has interesting exhibits of various kinds.

Beyond the immediate vicinity, we recommend the following attractions:

Heckscher Art Museum in Huntington, on Prime Avenue and Route 25A, was founded in 1920 and houses a small but excellent collection of American and European paintings. Open year round, Tuesday–Friday, 10:00 A.M. to 5:00 P.M., and Saturday and Sunday, 1:00 to 6:00 P.M.. Call 516-271-4440 for more information.

Vanderbilt Museum, near Northport, a 24-room Spanish Moroccan-style mansion on 43 wooded acres, is now a natural science museum and planetarium. See walk 13.

13

A Walk Through a Fanciful Museum/Estate
Vanderbilt Museum, Centerport

HOW TO GET THERE:

From uptown Manhattan: Take Cross Bronx Expressway to Throgs Neck Bridge, to Cross Island Parkway, to Long Island Expressway (495) to exit 51N (Deer Park Avenue). Take Deer Park Avenue (Route 231) north for six miles to Broadway and across Route 25A, where Broadway becomes Little Neck Road. The estate is on your right, behind white decorative walls, and is clearly marked. From midtown Manhattan: Midtown Tunnel to Long Island Expressway and follow same directions as above.

When you enter the imposing gates to the Vanderbilt Museum—once the fabled "Eagle's Nest" estate of one of America's most illustrious families—you are transported to an era of glamour, elegance, and privilege in a setting right out of a movie. Located on Long Island's North Shore, where many wealthy families built homes around the turn of the century, it includes the storybook, fanciful Vanderbilt mansion, a marine museum (housed in the whimsical-looking Hall of Fishes), a planetarium (added much later), six antique marble Corinthian columns in a semicircle near the entrance gate, a charming boathouse, and some 43 rolling acres overlooking Long Island Sound.

The estate was the home of William Kissam Vanderbilt II (1878–1944), great-grandson of "Commodore" Cornelius Vanderbilt of shipping and railroad fame. What he had begun in 1907 as a relatively modest six-room Japanese cottage was expanded over the years to a much grander 24 rooms in elaborate Spanish-Moroccan architectural style, with additional wings, courtyards, arcades, a tall, domed bell tower, a patio with reflecting pool, formal gardens, and a nearby ten-hole golf course and boathouse. When William Vanderbilt died in 1944, his will stipulated that the estate be donated for "the education and enjoyment of the public," to be used as a museum when his widow no longer wished to

THE VANDERBILT MUSEUM

live there. A man of surprisingly diverse interests—including architecture, art, anthropology, history, ornithology, ichthyology, sailing, auto racing, and aviation—he was a world traveler, explorer, sportsman, and collector. The visitor here will be fascinated and delighted by the array of things to view, from mounted animals (hunted by Vanderbilt himself), marine specimens, and dioramas, to fine paintings, rare objects, and unusual furniture—all personally collected by Vanderbilt. Unlike visits to many estates, this one is filled with surprises at every turn and should appeal to most anyone—including, or especially, children. You can walk through the Vanderbilt Marine Museum (Hall of Fishes) on your own and roam about the grounds freely. To visit the mansion itself you must join a guided tour; the guide provides unusually interesting tidbits of information about the life and times of Vanderbilt. The planetarium, built in 1971 on the site of what used to be the family tennis courts and now among the largest and best equipped in the country, is open to the public for regular sky shows Fridays at 8:30 P.M., Saturdays at 11:00 A.M., 1:00, 2:30,

4:00, and 8:30 P.M., and Sundays at 1:00, 2:30, and 4:00, as well as for public viewing after the evening sky shows, weather permitting. (Tickets are sold at the Planetarium box office half an hour before shows. For information call 516-757-7500.) In addition, the planetarium offers special programs such as live sky talks, school presentations, adult education courses in astronomy, meteorology, and navigation, and programs for the physically and mentally handicapped.

A visit to the Vanderbilt Museum is recommended for anyone interested in history, art, nature, zoology, or in just poking about and exploring a fascinating side of Americana in a beautiful natural setting with wonderful views of the water.

Children will surely be intrigued with the dioramas of natural scenes and the wide assortment of lifelike animals, including enormous crocodiles, whales, insects, and odd fish caught by Vanderbilt in many exotic places.

The mansion tour takes about 45 minutes, and is highly recommended. The rest of your visit depends on how much time you have to spend. The outdoor walk in the spacious grounds is pleasant, even if somewhat hilly. Wear comfortable shoes. There are no concessions or picnic facilities on the grounds, but plenty of cafés and restaurants can be found in Centerport or, even better, in nearby picturesque Northport.

The museum, which is open year-round Tuesdays–Saturdays, 10:00 A.M. to 4:00 P.M. and Sundays and holidays from noon to 5:00 P.M., is a popular destination on weekends (especially in summer and fall). We suggest you try to go during the week, if possible (unless you want to see a show at the planetarium). When we visited, on a brilliant Friday in mid-November, we were alone and enjoyed a private guided tour. For further museum information, call 516-261-5656.

THE WALK

After parking your car (near two imposing iron eagles), go to the visitors' reception center to buy your ticket, which includes everything except the planetarium. (When we were there admission fee was $4.00 for adults and $2.00 for children.) It is suggested that you first visit the Hall of Fishes. The oldest part of this original and eccentric building dates from 1922, but it was added on to at intervals, making it a sort of Moroccan potpourri. Made of white stucco and colorful tiles, it has four imposing, spiral columns next to the front door. The roof of this building was used by the Vanderbilts to tee off onto their private golf course just below. Inside, in one big room, are the colorful tropical marine specimens, as well as giant mounted fish, turtles, a whale, and other animals.

Return to the visitors' reception center for your guided tour of the mansion. (Tours are conducted regularly every 15 minutes and would not be difficult for average walkers.) You are first shown an interesting model of the entire mansion—including wings, courtyards, and gardens. The model will help you orient yourself in this extensive and labyrinthine structure. (Dollhouse enthusiasts may like this as much as anything on the tour!) Your next stop is the animal museum, a large dark room of dioramas displaying a variety of beasts and birds in lifelike settings, much like the Museum of Natural History.

Next you enter the house itself. The neo-Spanish-Moroccan style house is filled with original furnishings, memorabilia, objects, paintings, and artifacts that were all collected by William Vanderbilt on his travels in Europe and the Orient. The rooms have been kept just as they were when the family lived here. Vanderbilt acquired paintings and furniture based on his own personal tastes rather than on the advice of experts, and he placed them where he felt they looked best. Nothing has been moved or rearranged in any way. It is interesting to see the house in its genuine, lived-in arrangement, rather than as a museum, where things are placed according to periods and styles. The result, for such a grand house, is surprisingly intimate, warm, and friendly. We found the dining room, with its rustic furnishings, hand-carved wooden ceiling, and tile floors, particularly inviting. The bedrooms, including one that was frequently occupied by the Duke and Duchess of Windsor, who were close friends of the second Mrs. Vanderbilt, are cheerful and cozy, with bright fabrics and beautiful oriental rugs. One of the living rooms features a massive 2,000-pipe organ, which was installed in the 1920s for about $90,000. All of the rooms have views onto courtyards, formal gardens, or Long Island Sound, particularly in winter when the linden trees near the house have lost their leaves. Your last stop indoors is the insect and bird museum, where hundreds of species are displayed and identified. There are also many photographs of the Vanderbilts' exploits. At the end of the tour you are invited to explore the grounds further on your own. Walk through the formal gardens, including the charming English boxwood garden with its intricate patterns, see the reflecting pool and surrounding garden, and the rose garden—which is most fragrant and appealing in summer. You can wend your way down to the boathouse, a French-style building at the water's edge, where the Vanderbilts entertained afternoon yachting guests.

AFTER THE WALK

This is a scenic part of Long Island, not far from several places worth visiting: Teddy Roosevelt's home at Sagamore Hill (see walk 15), the picturesque town of Northport nearby and Eaton's Neck (see walk 16), or Caumsett State Park (see walk 12).

14

An Arboretum Outing
Planting Fields Arboretum, Oyster Bay

HOW TO GET THERE:

From uptown Manhattan: take Cross Bronx Expressway to Throgs Neck Bridge, to Cross Island Parkway, to Long Island Expressway and follow same directions as below.

From midtown Manhattan: Midtown Tunnel to the Long Island Expressway. Take the LIE to exit 39 North (Guinea Woods Road) to Route 25A (also called Northern Boulevard). Turn right on 25A. Pass C.W. Post College and make a left on Wolver Hollow Road (Route 4). Planting Fields Road will be a right turn about 2.5 miles away and the entrance is on the right.

An arboretum is not just a collection of trees. Planting Fields is a horticultural center for people who enjoy every sort of growing thing; there are greenhouses, plant collections, a wildflower walk, majestic trees, nature trails, sweeping lawns, a dwarf conifer garden, and in springtime a marvelous profusion of azaleas. In various seasons, the 409-acre estate offers just about every sort of plant-life environment: about 160 acres are developed and the rest is kept as a natural habitat of fields and woods. For this reason, the most varied interests in growing or planting rare trees, herbs, or unusual plants can be satisfied. And if you just want a nice place to walk, the Planting Fields Arboretum is a simply beautiful estate-like place to wander.

This was once the private estate of William Robertson Coe. His home, Coe Hall, an elegant example of Elizabethan-style architecture, is occasionally used for concerts, other cultural events, and school activities. The grounds, which are now under the jurisdiction of the Long Island State Park Commission, are kept meticulously (in the developed section), with changing displays and identifying tags on trees, shrubbery, and flower beds. The wilder part is crisscrossed with trails. All sorts of courses in horticulture, painting, photography, or ecology are offered at the

DIRECTIONS TO
PLANTING FIELDS
ARBORETUM

arboretum, as are guided tours of the greenhouses and grounds, but you can also just go and wander about on your own. A brochure is offered at the headquarters, describing over 7,500 specimens in the Herbarium. A self-guided tour booklet and map are also available.

While the arboretum is open year-round, you should phone (516-922-9200) for definite information on what you will see when you get there. Planting Fields is open daily throughout the year, from 10:00 A.M. to 5:00 P.M. mid-April through October, and until 4:30 P.M. November through mid-April. A small admission fee is charged except during weekdays in winter, when it is free; children under 12 are always free. We recommend this walk for people of all ages. Children will find plenty to interest them, from natural to cultivated areas and perhaps their first greenhouse. There are many quite flat areas, although there are some longish distances from one thing to the next. But you'll enjoy even a short walk in these flowering sweet-smelling acres. There are no refreshments, nor is picnicking allowed.

THE WALK

The arboretum is divided into several sections. You can plan to "do" them all, or focus on separate parts. Here is what you can see outdoors: The grounds have majestic trees, many of which are the largest of their kind on Long Island. There are lindens, tulip trees, cedars-of-Lebanon, beech, elms, Sargent weeping hemlocks, among many others.

There are azaleas and rhododendrons galore. Some 600 plants make up this collection, which is famous throughout the East. (Late April or early May is a good time to visit for this reason.) In spring you'll also see daffodils, magnolias, forsythia, weeping cherries, dogwood, flowering crabapples, lilacs, and wisterias. Summertime finds the grounds filled with blooming mountain laurel, and changing annual border flowers. Each season has its beauties at the arboretum; in fall chrysanthemums and franklinia are set off by the brilliant foliage.

The five-acre Synoptic Garden, a specialty here, is an unusual arrangement of ornamental shrubs and small trees. The plants are alphabetically arranged, each identified with a label describing its family, country of origin, and botanical and common names.

The Dwarf Conifer Garden is of particular interest to those with small gardens themselves; it features a wide range of miniature or dwarf plants and bulbs. The nature trails, on the other hand, are just as rough and natural as the gardens are manicured. Enjoy the woodsy walks and the birds you spot as you stroll. You should get the map at the desk before leaving the parking area, for this is an extensive place.

The indoor greenhouses, always an elegant addition to an estate, are just as you would expect: filled with bright colors and pretty patterns, these are familiar, rather than exotic, plants. Winter displays include poinsettias, cyclamen, and camellias. March brings the English spring garden and a profusion of orchids. In April an Easter display and cactus plants are featured, and in May, geraniums of different types are exhibited. The summer finds the greenhouses filled with bedding plants such as begonias and impatiens, and in autumn chrysanthemums and orchids are shown. Occasional displays feature oddities such as banana and coffee plants.

It is, of course, the grounds that make this walk special, but a visit to the greenhouses is a nice way to complete your outing.

AFTER THE WALK

The village of Oyster Bay is a charming little community, once a whaling town. Many of the original buildings still exist. You can visit a number of historic houses there and poke into the boutiques and restaurants that line the short Main Street area.

Not far away is Sagamore Hill, Teddy Roosevelt's extraordinary summer home and the nearby gardens (if you haven't had your fill of garden walks). See walk 15 for details about Sagamore Hill.

15

A Visit to Teddy Roosevelt's Sagamore Hill
Oyster Bay

HOW TO GET THERE:

From uptown Manhattan: Take Cross Bronx Expressway to Throgs Neck Bridge, to Cross Island Parkway, to Long Island Expressway to exit 41 North. Take Route 106 north to Oyster Bay, turn right at the third traffic light, follow signs to Sagamore Hill on Cove Neck Road. (The site is well marked.)
From midtown Manhattan: Midtown Tunnel to Long Island Expressway and follow same directions as above.

Sagamore Hill is neither a mansion nor a grand reminder of long-gone elegance. It is a large but unpretentious and entirely charming family home high above a cove at Oyster Bay, and it is both historically and scenically delightful. There is lots to look at, from the rambling, spacious house and veranda, to the historical museum down the garden path, to a magnificent view in all directions. The atmosphere is quiet and reminiscent; you get quite a feeling of Teddy Roosevelt as you wander through the house and examine the wild game heads and skins on the walls, the mementoes of travel, the dark paneled rooms all with vistas of the sea. At the Old Orchard Museum you'll find historic exhibitions relating to Teddy's political career, his personal life, and to the six Roosevelt children. A visit to Sagamore Hill can also include driving about a mile to his grave site, which adjoins a museum, formal gardens, and a bird sanctuary administered by the Audubon Society.

Sagamore Hill was built by Roosevelt during 1884 and 1885, after the death of his first wife. When it was completed—entirely to his specifications ("I wished a big piazza," he wrote, "where we could sit in rocking chairs and look at the sunset . . ."), he moved in with his sister Anna and his small daughter, Alice. Soon afterward he remarried; three of his six children were born at

Sagamore Hill. Here T. R. spent the rest of his life, entertaining political and international guests, and enjoying his family until his death in 1919. "After all," he wrote, "fond as I am of the White House and much though I have appreciated these years in it, there isn't any place in the world like home—like Sagamore Hill, where things are our own, with our own associations."

For some 30 years Sagamore Hill was home to the Roosevelts, whose large and cheerful family were of endless interest to the public. Newspapers maintained a vigil at Sagamore Hill, chronicling the family's outdoor pastimes; T.R. could frequently be seen playing with his children, hiking, swimming, and riding horseback across his property. What he described as "the joy of life" was part of his national image of family man, sportsman, and statesman. Some of that feeling is evident to the visitor. It is not hard to imagine the Roosevelt family of the turn of the century bustling through these comfortable rooms and enjoying the expansive veranda.

We suggest that you visit Sagamore Hill and the surrounding sites during the week, if you can. A popular spot, it gets a heavy dose of tourists, particularly at vacation times. All of the buildings are open all year (closed on major holidays) from 9:00 A.M. to 5:00 P.M. There is a small admission charge. The trails at the

Sanctuary are open from 2:00 to 5:00 daily. There are no refreshments at any of the sites. Picnicking is not allowed, but Oyster Bay, nearby, has many eating places.

This is a good outing for walkers of all levels, as it is flat and has easy footing; but there are stairs. We particularly recommend it for older visitors, who will enjoy many of the historical connotations and will perhaps recall some of the events and personalities that seem to come alive as you walk through T.R.'s house and grounds.

For further information on Sagamore Hill, call 516-922-4447.

THE WALK

Sagamore Hill is a 23-room Victorian house made of frame and brick. The downstairs includes a large center hall, a library that served as T.R.'s office, Mrs. Roosevelt's drawing room, a dining room, kitchen, and a spacious north room added in 1905. This room in particular reflects T.R.'s personality; here you'll see the hunting trophies, the books, flags, paintings, and mementoes of his life. On the second floor are the charming bedrooms and the nursery, and don't miss the giant porcelain bathtub! On the top floor you'll find the gun room, housing T.R.'s collection of hunting arms, though he also used it to entertain his friends in privacy. There are rooms for cooks and maids, a sewing room, and a schoolroom. Also of interest is the president's bedroom as it looked in his pre-Harvard days. Throughout you'll notice bulging bookcases, paintings, and memorabilia that are all of interest.

Outdoors you'll find landscaped gardens, the Roosevelt family pet cemetery, and a path to the Old Orchard Museum. Opened to the public in 1966, the museum contains three permanent exhibits, a gallery, a projection room, a large collection of Roosevelt memorabilia, including a number of documentaries and motion pictures about T.R. and the family. T.R.'s son built the house called Old Orchard in 1938; in 1960 it was added to the Sagamore Hill National Historic Site.

You can return to your car after visiting these two sites and the grounds, and drive down the hill for about a mile to the Sanctuary and T.R.'s grave. Here you'll find a series of bird-watching trails, some formal gardens, and the grave. The Sanctuary also has exhibits, bird attracting devices, and plantings. You can have guided tours, too, by calling 516-WA2-3200.

AFTER THE WALK

This part of the North Shore is strikingly beautiful, and any one of the necks jutting out into Long Island Sound has great views, or beach, or harbor to explore. There are also several pleasant towns to wander through, including Cold Spring Harbor and Northport. We suggest exploring Oyster Bay, which has other interesting sites, including Raynham Hall, a 1740s house that contained the British headquarters during the Revolutionary War (call 516-922-6808 for information), and Planting Fields Arboretum (see walk 14). Not far away is the Vanderbuit Mansion (see walk 13), if you want to see two quite dissimilar estates in one day.

16

A Breakwater and Beach Walk
on the Sound
Eatons Neck

HOW TO GET THERE:
Long Island Expressway to exit 51, which is Route 231. Go north on 231, passing Northern State Parkway intersection. At Route 25 (Jericho Turnpike) get on Route 10, which will take you into Northport. To reach Eatons Neck, take Ocean Avenue, then Asharoken Road to Eatons Neck Road to the end.

Anyone who has spent time on the seacoast remembers the fun of hopping, running, or strolling on the long breakwaters that stretch into the harbors of so many New England towns. We were happy to discover one that is only about an hour from the city, and on a lovely stretch of pebbly beach, too. The breakwater on this oddly shaped beach is really on the neck of a neck; Eatons Neck is a peninsula that stretches out into the waters of Long Island Sound north of Northport, and the beach itself a long, skinny strip of sand and rocks that juts out from the end of it. When we visited (not in summer) there were one or two fishermen casting from the rocks, and one solitary stroller with his dog. The air was fresh and salty, the beach filled with wonderful pebbles of a hundred hues, and the breakwater quite a challenge.

The stroller informed us that people enjoy a sport here that they call "bouldering." It consists of jumping from the top of one giant stone to the next, despite spaces, odd surfaces, and pointed rocks. We can't give you a competitive time to complete your breakwater bouldering, but we do recommend that you be careful. Enjoy yourself on as much of the long breakwater as you can do, and then set off to walk on the beach alongside and beyond the rest of the way.

The beach itself is a typical North Shore beach, covered densely with pebbles, occasional shells, and driftwood. When we walked

NORTHPORT and EATONS NECK

it in the fall and spring, we found it pleasantly empty of trash. The beachcomber can pick up little rose-quartz stones, skipping stones, irregularly shaped driftwood, and the usual flotsam and jetsam.

In order to reach this beach you will have driven through an unusually charming North Shore village called Northport. We recommend that you return to it after you've enjoyed the beach walk, and explore the bustling marina and main street.

Northport, which was once known as Cowharbor, was founded in 1656. It has had a flourishing history as a shipbuilding and fishing village, and then as a summer resort for New Yorkers at the turn of the century. The harbor, which still supports crabbing and oystering, is a busy recreational boaters' haven, and the charming town green with its circular bandstand and paths leading to the wooden wharf will remind you of an old-fashioned seaside setting from earlier days. The main street shops cater to visiting boaters, as well as to the recently arrived residents who have spruced up the many original and antique houses. There are restaurants and ice cream parlors and boutiques galore, but the town has not succumbed to commercial cuteness and is a very pleasant place to stroll. If you like looking at old houses of various architectural styles, don't miss Bayview, the waterfront street of 19th-century homes.

We do not recommend this walk in midsummer, unless you pick a rainy day or want to swim and don't mind crowds of people. If you go early in the morning or toward evening you'll see a good variety of birds at the tip of the neck, which was once a wildlife preserve.

It is windy on the neck, so bundle up. Anyone planning to do the breakwater should wear sneakers. You can buy all the refreshments you'd ever want in Northport, but the beach is a good spot for a picnic, too. If you're a birder, bring binoculars. Many waterfowl and migrating birds like this remote tip of land.

The sand spit itself is totally flat and the sand is not soft, so that any walker of any age can enjoy it. The breakwater is hard going and only for the most fit, but this is a good hike for a family to do together, as the energetic ones can hop along the rocks, while the more sedate can walk beside them.

THE WALK

Leave your car in the lot at the end of Eatons Neck Road, where you will see the boat launching area and a small brick building. Walk straight out toward the beach. The breakwater begins about .25 mile out into the beach. Off-season you'll be strolling along a quite deserted stretch, or hopping the odd-shaped rocks of the breakwater that protects the bay harbor from storm and tide. From the end of the breakwater you can keep going farther and farther from the village and out to the lonely tip of sand, pebbles, and sea gulls. The distances are not great: the entire walk is perhaps two miles (but don't forget you have to go back, too). The breakwater is about .5 to .75 of a mile of that two miles.

AFTER THE WALK

We have already suggested that you explore the marina and village of Northport. You can also visit several nearby attractions: the Vanderbilt Mansion (see walk 13); Caumsett (see walk 12); or start back toward New York and stop at Teddy Roosevelt's wonderful Sagamore Hill (see walk 15).

THE HUDSON VALLEY (EAST)

17

Over and Under a Dam
The New Croton Dam, Cortland

HOW TO GET THERE:

From Manhattan take the Henry Hudson Parkway north and continue on the Saw Mill River Parkway. Follow signs for Route 9 north and Tarrytown. Continue on Route 9 north past North Tarrytown, Scarborough, and Ossining. You'll see a sign for Croton-on-Hudson. Take second exit, following signs for Route 129. Stay on 129 for about four miles. The entrance to Croton Gorge Park is on your right. You can either enter the park, cross the wooden bridge, and leave your car there; or, continue on Route 129 for about .3 mile, take Croton Dam Road on your right, and park your car just before reaching the dam.

It's been hailed as the eighth wonder of the world, the most beautiful of all dams, the one with the most impressive masonry work. It's been praised, sung about, immortalized in verse and on canvas, and made into a national historic site. It's been walked over and photographed. The Croton Dam, majestically situated high amid the rolling Westchester hills, continues to impress the visitor. Crossing it on foot and then walking down into the park below—the undeveloped Croton Gorge Park—to get another good view of it, makes for an unusual and interesting walk.

A bit of history should be kept in mind at this spectacular site. The dam—called the New Croton Dam to distinguish it from its predecessor—supplies much of New York City's water, some 400 million gallons out of the almost 2 billion gallons the city needs daily. During the 1830s, after New York City was devastated by cholera and fire, the city planners realized that the city's growing population could no longer rely on the existing water supply (from local springs and wells) and that a new dam and aqueduct would have to be built to bring in more water. The Croton River, with its various branches and abundant, pure, and wholesome water, seemed a good choice for the creation of these waterworks.

The first dam, worked on by Irish laborers fleeing the potato famine, was completed in 1842. However, some years later it became apparent that a new dam would have to be built to accommodate the ever-expanding city. After many preliminary studies, the northern end of the Croton River watershed was chosen for a high masonry dam and work on the project was finally begun in 1892. Highways, homes, and hotels had to be relocated to build roads, bridges, and superstructures. Italian laborers—providing expertise in stone masonry—were imported from southern Italy and Sicily. Unfortunately, a variety of engineering mishaps and labor unrest due to the miserable conditions caused the work to drag on. On April 1, 1900, the workers staged a huge wildcat strike. They came roaring down the hill, brandishing knives and threatening to blow up the dam. The Westchester National Guard and Teddy Roosevelt's Rough Riders were called in to quell the riot. After further delays, the final stone of the dam was laid on December 15, 1906, and the dam officially opened in January 1907 amid great celebration. Instead of the intended five years and $4 million, it took almost 15 years to build and cost almost $12 million. At 297 feet high and 2,168 feet long, it was the largest dam in the world at that time. The amount of masonry used to build it was said to be equal to that used in building the Great Pyramid of Cheops!

On this walk, we recommend you take binoculars, a sketch pad, or a camera to record the scenery on both sides of the dam. There are no designated picnic spots or public facilities either in the park or on the Old Croton Aqueduct trail nearby, but opportunities for picnicking are not lacking. If you intend to make this a longer walk, bring drinking water and wear solid shoes.

Although the actual crossing of the dam is hardly rigorous (and is fairly short), the walk up and down and around it is more tiring. Those who don't like hills might choose to limit their walk accordingly. If you decide to venture forth on the Old Croton Aqueduct Pathway, you'll find the going easy and basically flat. This is an all-season walk. If you plan to continue on the old Croton Aqueduct trail, arrange for transportation somewhere along this lengthy route. The Croton Gorge Park is never crowded because of its lack of facilities (we were there on a Labor Day weekend and saw only a couple of people).

To take the full old Croton Aqueduct walk, pick up the walk directory from the New York State Parks, Taconic Region, Staatsburg, New York, 12580 or call 914-889-4100.

THE WALK

Park your car either inside the Croton Gorge Park (no fee) and begin your walk from there, or drive directly to the dam, leaving your car by the side of the road. If you've chosen the first option, walk across a picturesque wooden bridge and up through the park entrance, turning right onto Route 129 and going up the hill for a short distance. Go right at Croton Dam Road and proceed to the dam.

Crossing the dam won't take very long—it's only about .3 mile—but you'll want to stop and enjoy the views on both sides. On your right you can admire the rolling hills of the Croton River Valley. The meandering river is not too visible because of the dense woodlands surrounding it, but you can observe the reservoir water rushing through the dam's spillway into it. (Unfortunately, you can also see junk that people have thrown down from the dam walkway!) On the reservoir side—the left as you walk across the dam—you see a peaceful, large lake with an occasional fisherman's rowboat (fishing is allowed only with permit). From here you can admire the masonry that has been so praised. You'll be awestruck by the impressive engineering feat this dam represents. After you have crossed the dam you'll see a path (with two large rocks in front) immediately to the right. This marks the beginning of the Old Croton Aqueduct Trail, which goes all the way to 173rd Street in upper Manhattan, some 32 miles, crossing woodlands, meadows, estates, abandoned farms, and suburbs. The Old Croton Aqueduct, finished in the 1840s along with the Old Croton Dam, was taken out of service to New York City in 1955 and has since been used by walkers, joggers, bikers, equestrians, and cyclists. You might choose to walk along this trail for whatever distance you feel up to, remembering that you'll have to retrace your steps. This path is a naturalist's delight. In spring, blooming dogwood, mountain laurel, and other shrubs proliferate. In summer you can pick blackberries. There are wooded areas of pine, oak, hemlock, and mulberry where you might spot a deer, raccoon, or rabbit. Birders can observe cardinals, red-winged blackbirds, robins, crows, and pheasants.

If your time is limited, start on this trail, walk for a few moments, then leave the trail, turning right and going down a fairly steep grassy slope into Croton Gorge Park. (There is no actual path leading you to the park, only the evidence of others who have made their own trail.) Walk across the meadow to the dam and view it from this new perspective. You can especially appreciate the details of stonework from this angle. Then walk along the river for a while, if you are willing to make your own way over rocks and through woods. There are no trails in this park: it is completely undeveloped, with the exception of the small parking area and a modest children's playground off to the side.

AFTER THE WALK

We have several suggestions, depending on your time and energy level. You can combine this walk with walk 21. The aqueduct goes through the Rockefeller State Park Preserve, less than ten miles south.

A pleasant drive along the reservoir (Croton Lake) is enjoyable—particularly in fall with the spectacular foliage. Drive across the dam and continue on the road (Croton Lake Road) all the way around. It becomes a dirt road, but is fairly wide, scenic, and uncrowded. You pass by two bridges: cross at the third (for a longer drive, keep going straight), and get back onto Route 129. The lake is to your left at all times. Eventually you will cross another bridge over the lake. This circular drive is about nine miles long.

Croton Point Park is an especially scenic spot and worth seeing, if only to admire its spectacular situation on the Hudson. Unlike Croton Gorge Park, this is a somewhat developed area with playing fields, a family campground (off to the side), picnic tables at water's edge, a playground, and a small bathing beach—if you care to swim in the Hudson. Situated on a dramatic point that juts out into the river, it commands great views of the entire region on all sides: Haverstraw and Hook Mountain lie directly across; historic Tarrytown lighthouse, the Tappan Zee Bridge, and New York City skyline can be seen to the far south on a clear day. On the other side of this peninsula lies Croton Bay with its surrounding tidal marsh where loons, egrets, or cormorants live. There is good fishing along the banks of the river because of the rich marsh habitat. Fishermen we talked to said they hoped to catch striped bass, perch, Atlantic sturgeon, or weakfish.

The park has great expanses of grassy fields with willows and locust trees and a nearby conifer forest. It is open daily from 8:00 A.M. to dusk, and there is a small fee for parking. Pets are not allowed.

The Audubon Sanctuary at Brinton Brook northwest of the dam is also a nice spot for birding.

18

A Walk Through Sleepy Hollow Cemetery
Tarrytown

HOW TO GET THERE:

From midtown, east side: F.D.R. Drive to Major Deegan Expressway north, which becomes the New York Thruway. Exit at Route 9, just before the Tappan Zee Bridge (exit 9) at Tarrytown. Go north on Route 9, which is Broadway. Go through Tarrytown; the cemetery is on your right.
From midtown, west side: Henry Hudson Parkway which becomes Saw Mill River Parkway, to New York State Thruway, follow directions above.

Sleepy Hollow Cemetery is a rare graveyard—neither dismal nor unattractive. Its rolling terrain and giant trees shelter the graves of all sorts of people—from early Dutch settlers of this Hudson River area to the great robber barons and philanthropists of the last century to the most famous of the area's native sons, Washington Irving, whose lovely home, Sunnyside, is nearby.

The walks through this cemetery are as long or as short as you wish to make them; at every turn you'll come across lovely vistas, interesting markers, and even a gurgling river with a wooden bridge. The people at the main gate will give you a map outlining (very roughly indeed) where to locate the most famous graves. But if you enjoy this type of walk, you'll find yourself wandering more or less at random, among the giant mausoleums of the late 19th century, the old sandstone markers of the early Dutch and English settlers, and the charming iron-fenced plots of early families. While walking through a cemetery or making grave rubbings may be an acquired taste, we found this particular site filled with interest—historical, scenic, and visual, for many of the monuments are quite extraordinary. There are Greek Revival mausoleums, obelisks and columns surmounted with flying angels, as well as hundreds of more common markers. The cemetery is uncrowded and very large, so you can walk about at will, meeting,

A WALK THROUGH SLEEPY HOLLOW CEMETERY

LOOK FOR:
1. OLD CHURCH YARD
   and
   OLD DUTCH CHURCH
2. WASHINGTON IRVING'S GRAVE
3. REVOLUTIONARY WAR MONUMENT
4. DELAVAN MONUMENT
5. ANDREW CARNEGIE'S GRAVE
6. SAMUEL GOMPER'S GRAVE
7. WILLIAM ROCKEFELLER'S MAUSOLEUM

S
E
W
N

POCANTICO RIVER

SLEEPY HOLLOW AVENUE

SLEEPY HOLLOW CEMETERY

CENTRAL

MAIN GATE

LINCOLN AVE.

TERRACE AVE.

ENTRANCE

OLD CHURCH YARD
1.

BROADWAY

ROUTE 9

To TARRYTOWN

south
1 mile to
Sunnyside

Sleepy Hollow Restorations

To OSSINING

North 9 miles
to Van Cortlandt Manor

as we did, only gardeners carefully tending the flowering shrubbery and grassy hillsides. Washington Irving called the area "a sequestered glen . . . one of the quietest places in the whole world . . ." Fortunately, his words still seem true

We recommend this outing to those with an interest in history and a taste for this special kind of walk. (Most probably this group will not include children.) The walk is somewhat hilly and can be very long, depending on where you park and how far you wish to go, but for the moderately fit visitor it's an easy outing. The walkways are mostly soft, though some are paved. You should not bring pets or radios or other noise-makers, as there is a sense of silence you wouldn't want to disturb. If you like making grave rubbings, by all means bring paper and the soft crayon sold at most art supply stores especially for this purpose. (Several good monuments for rubbings are identified below.)

Sleepy Hollow Cemetery is open daily from 8:00 A.M. to 4:30 P.M. year round. It is particularly pretty in spring and fall, but there is no reason you shouldn't do the walk on a coolish summer day. The Old Dutch Church, however, is open only on Sundays (when you can also take a tour).

THE WALK

The Old Dutch Church stands at one end of the cemetery, surrounded by the oldest graves. The rushing little river, the Pocantico, is crossed by Irving's "Headless Horseman Bridge" just below. The rest of the cemetery's oldest sections lie between Broadway (Route 9) and the river; across the little river is a newer (and less interesting) section.

You can park either near the Old Dutch Church or within the cemetery along one of the winding roads. You can begin your walk at the Old Church (as shown on our map), or you can start at the main gate, where you pick up your map from the office. (The map is almost illegible, but it might help you find your way from one walkway to the next.)

If you start at the church (1), take a look first at this very old landmark. It was built by Frederick Philipse (see Philipsburg Manor described below) in 1697 or 1699 for his family and the tenants of the manor house. The cupola contains the original bell, making it almost 300 years old. There are not many landmarks in our country of that antiquity. The legend reads "If God be for us, who can be against us?" Both Philipse and his wife, who was named Catherine Van Cortland (see Van Cortland Manor below) are buried beneath the chancel of the church. If you can't get in, peak through the windows at the simple and charming architecture.

The graves in the churchyard are among the oldest at Sleepy Hollow. Here you'll see the same names many times, with markers bearing the traditional weeping willow design. (Most are too decayed for grave rubbings, though one or two have clear-cut carving.)

Next, seek out Washington Irving's fenced-in family plot. Try walking northward on Lincoln Avenue, to Crane, to Paulding. Irving's grave (2) is in a charming little garden with about 50 family graves surrounding it. There is a giant tree sheltering them all, and a wrought-iron gate and fence encircling both tree and graves. Irving, author of some of America's best loved classics ("The Legend of Sleepy Hollow" among them), was both an author and diplomat. He lived from 1783 to 1859. His grave and garden around it seem appropriately old and charming.

If you walk on, following the winding road (unnamed), you'll come to the Revolutionary War monument, which is unremarkable except for its beautiful hillside location with a distant view. (3)

Directly behind it is the Delavan monument (4), a strikingly tall column with a figure high atop. David Delavan (1757–1835) is buried there, surrounded with giant sculpted angels. It is a site worth noticing. Just behind it, in the Hawes plot, is a good grave rubbing monument with a traditional willow design. It might say "Cornelia Amy," but it's hard to read.

As you walk between the locusts and cypresses and evergreen trees, you'll pass some extraordinary mausoleums and chapels, built in a variety of classical and romantic styles. Turn down toward the river for a walk along its rippling banks on Sleepy Hollow Road. Eventually you'll come to another road up the hill (away from the river) called Cascade Avenue.

If you make your way steadily up and follow the paths you'll come to two more interesting graves: first, and somewhat hidden from the walkway, is the Celtic cross marking the grave of Andrew

Carnegie. Carnegie, who lived from 1835 to 1919, was the great industrialist (founder of Carnegie Steel) and philanthropist who built Carnegie Hall, many public libraries, and gave away some $350 million for public institutions. His grave is in a small circular garden, reached from the walkway by a short stone path. It is in the style of a fine Celtic cross with many carved markings, and it is beautifully set and neither ostentatious nor grand.

Just across the roadway from this spot is the grave of Samuel Gompers (6), the labor leader and first president of the American Federation of Labor. Gompers, who died in 1924, has a distinctly unfancy grave marker, placed there by the union.

Finally, make your way up to the crest of a hill where you'll find the huge mausoleum of William Rockefeller. This massive neoclassical building has Ionic columns and inscribed walls like a public institution; other members of the Rockefeller family are also buried around it. It sits, in great splendor, in a circular space with a giant hedge surrounding it. William Rockefeller (1841–1922) was a brother and associate of John D. and a codeveloper of Standard Oil.

You can continue wandering on your own, of course. Among the other graves of interest are those of Mark Hellinger, for whom a Broadway theater was named; Major Bowes, the 1940s radio personality; and Walter Chrysler, the American auto industrialist. However, you might find, as we did, that many of the most interesting graves are those bearing unfamiliar names.

AFTER THE WALK

The entire Tarrytown region is filled with interesting historic sites, most in some way related to the legendary Sleepy Hollow. Here are some of the side visits you might want to take after your walk.

Sleepy Hollow Restorations: This is a collection of beautifully restored homes, all furnished in period antiques. You'll get a taste of what life was once like in the Hudson River Valley. Among the restored buildings are:

Sunnyside: Washington Irving's charming home, still maintained in his style, with desk, wood stove, etc. Here you can take a tour and stroll through the gardens to the banks of the Hudson.

Van Cortland Manor: The home of one of the Hudson Valley's

earliest prominent families, this is a fine example of architecture of the Dutch period, with its sweeping staircase, porch, and graceful garden. There are demonstrations of manor life (à la Williamsburg), including colonial crafts.

Philipsburg Manor: This fine job of restoration returns an entire manor—from farmhouse to garden to mills—to its original appearance, between 1720 and 1750. It is most appealing, with bare floors, whitewashed walls, and simple charm.

In our opinion, the entire restoration is slightly marred by period costumes on the guides, tours, educational films, and other "restoration-itis," apparently aimed at schoolchildren. However, if you go to Tarrytown, Sunnyside alone is well worth the visit. The restorations are open from 10:00 A.M. to 5:00 P.M. daily, closed major holidays and Tuesdays in winter. Call 914-631-8200 for specific information, as well as admission prices, which vary according to the number of places you visit. The least expensive ticket is $5.00 for adults, $3.00 for children, which allows you to visit one restoration project.

Lyndhurst: A Gothic Revival castle, the home of Jay Gould the financier, is also just down the street from the cemetery in Tarrytown (at 635 South Broadway). This odd, 19th-century palace overlooking the Hudson has a treasure trove of furniture, decorations, Tiffany glass, silver, rugs, fine paintings, and trompe l'oeil designs.

Union Church, Pocantico Hills: A real find among all of this history is the small Union Church just up the hill from Tarrytown. Here, nestled in a pretty village where the palatial Rockefeller estate is located, is a lovely ivy-covered church housing stained-glass windows by Marc Chagall and a wonderful rose window by Matisse. Seven of these stunning windows, mostly memorials to various members of the Rockefeller family, are devoted to Old Testament prophets and are amazingly like Chagall's paintings with their brilliant colors and biblical designs. Admission is by donation. To reach the church turn up the hill (away from the river) at the center of Tarrytown on Route 448 and follow the winding road to Pocantico Hills. The church is open from 1:00 to 4:00 P.M. on Wednesdays, Thursdays, and Fridays, 2:00 to 4:00 P.M. on Sundays, from April to December. Information is available by calling 914-631-8200.

19

A Walk Through a Hemlock Woodland Gorge

Mianus River Gorge Wildlife and Botanical Preserve, Westchester County

HOW TO GET THERE:

From uptown Manhattan, take the Major Deegan Expressway to Cross County Parkway, to the Hutchinson River Parkway, to Route 684 north. Exit at Route 22 north and follow signs for Bedford Village. From the center of the village follow signs for Route 172. Turn right at Long Ridge Road (where you will also see a sign for Stamford, Conn.), continue for about a mile, turn right on Millers Mill Road, and follow signs to Mianus River Gorge Wildlife Refuge and Botanical Preserve.

An excursion to the Mianus River Gorge Wildlife Refuge and Botanical Preserve is ideal if you are seeking an unspoiled wilderness in relatively close proximity to New York City. Located less than 40 miles northeast of Manhattan in a rural section of Westchester County, the park includes about 450 acres of pristine woodland along the banks and gorge of the Mianus River. The gorge is a deep ravine that was carved out by a great sheet of ice some 10,000 or more years ago. The name of the river comes from Myanos, a local Indian chief the white settlers met when they first arrived in the 17th century.

This is an inviting spot for a quiet walk in a natural and tranquil sylvan setting. The only sounds you hear are those of birds (there are more than 150 species), or the rushing river in the ravine, or a nearby gurgling brook. There are five miles of foot trails that go up and down over hilly terrain, amid a rich variety of plant and animal life. In spring you walk among masses of wildflowers: wild geraniums, pink lady's slippers, rue anemones, marsh marigolds, dwarf ginseng, and cardinal flowers, to name a few of the 250 or so species that proliferate. The dense, dark evergreen forest alternates with leafy, airy woodlands of maples, beeches, tulip trees, and dogwoods, so that you go in and out of shadows, with varying degrees of sunlight filtering through the foliage.

The conservation-minded founders of the preserve decided not to provide outdoor recreation in a traditional park setting with playing fields and picnic facilities. In fact, there are a number of restrictions, which no doubt account for the fact that the park is uncrowded and without the usual distractions: no fires, smoking, dogs (even on leashes), picnics, hunting, boating, or camping.

The walk in this preserve is wonderful for urban dwellers who seldom have the opportunity to experience nature firsthand. We recommend it also for adventuresome children who love to explore and who should be intrigued by an enormous hemlock reputed to be more than 300 years old. For those who prefer organized or interpretive walks, weekly Sunday afternoon outings (sponsored by the active Mianus River Gorge Conservation Committee) are held at 2:00 P.M. Participants set out through the gorge with a naturalist who can talk about birds, geology, local Indian culture, and natural history. On Saturday mornings you can join another group for such things as searching for mushrooms, studying the ecology of the gorge, photographing wildflowers, or viewing the winter landscape. (For further information, call 914-234-3455.) Although the trails are quite hilly, they are not too difficult to manage if you proceed at a leisurely pace. However, we do not recommend them for those who find climbing arduous.

The gorge walk is lovely at all times of the year, although the preserve is officially closed from December 1 to April 1. Some sections of the trails are shut down during the winter, but you can still enjoy walking through the snow in other parts of the park. Late spring is a wonderful time to go, particularly if you are partial to wildflowers; summer is pleasant, with warm breezes on the hillside above the gorge; and, of course, the autumn trees are resplendent.

We suggest you equip yourself with sturdy walking shoes, since the trails can be fairly rugged, though well-maintained. Save your picnic for after your visit to Mianus Gorge.

THE WALK

The approach to the preserve sets the tone for what is to come. From Millers Mill Road you drive along Miller's Mill Dam with its impressive cascade, bearing to the left and following discreet signs to the entrance of the preserve. Park your car and at the shelter pick up a trail map, which gives you a good description of where you are going. Basically you will be staying on one trail, which is marked in red going out and blue coming back. There are detours worth making along the way, all of which are indicated on the trail guide.

As you start on your walk, you are struck by the silence around you. After a moment you will see a small wooden bench on your left, slightly off the trail, with a view overlooking the beginning of the gorge. This bench, called the Lucy D.S. Adams Memorial Bench, was placed there for those who cannot walk the trails but want to enjoy this special environment.

You proceed over a soft carpet of pine needles, leaves, and mosses, always following the well-marked trail. You cross a charming little stone bridge over a brook with masses of ferns and beeches alongside. The path leads you up and down hills, with occasional views of the gorge below. About a half hour into the walk you will come to a place where you make a sharp turn up a rather steep hill with random stone steps and gnarled tree roots. You are now on your way to the "Hemlock Cathedral," a 20-acre site of tall, majestic trees atop a hill. This is a quiet place. The sunlight filtering through the trees creates the impression of the interior of a Gothic church. You pass a beech grove and a wild-ginger colony. You'll see a series of lovely old stone walls along the way that marked the boundaries between farms of long ago. A recommended detour is Hobby Hill Quarry, where mica, quartz, and feldspar were mined during the 18th century. We also suggest you take a few minutes and follow the signs for the reservoir view. The Havemeyer Falls, one of the main sights of the excursion, are finally reached after you go down a fairly rugged, rocky path that can be slippery with wet leaves and roots. Follow the sound of the falls as they cascade over the rocks, and you are there. This gentle waterfall may not be dramatic, but is a lovely spot to stop for a moment. If you follow the trail to the lookout point at the end, you will be rewarded with a fine view of the entire region, including the reservoir and gorge. Retrace your steps, following the blue markers back to your starting point. The entire walk (about five miles if you include the various detours) is no more than three hours, if taken at a leisurely pace. It's impossible to get lost, as everything is well marked.

AFTER THE WALK

Nearby Bedford Village is worth a short visit. Surrounded by elegant 19th-century frame houses that line the pleasant, shaded streets, it is clustered around a lovely village green, like many traditional New England towns. Don't miss the charming Carpenter Gothic Presbyterian church and the 18th-century courthouse, now a small museum.

Caramoor, the impressive Mediterranean-style country estate of a New York lawyer, banker, and art collector, Walter Tower Rosen, and his wife, Lucie Bigelow Dodge, is only a few minutes' drive from Bedford Village. (Follow Route 22 to the junction of Girdle Ridge Road, about 3.4 miles, where you'll see a small sign for Caramoor. Turn right and continue for about .5 mile, to the entrance of the estate.) Built in the 1930s to house the couple's extensive collection of European art and furniture, in 1970 it was opened to the public as a museum and center for music and the arts. It now hosts an internationally known music festival. The house includes some 55 rooms (only 19 of the rooms are open for public viewing), all decorated in authentic period pieces from medieval monasteries of Spain and Italy, palaces and chateaux of France, and from China. The house is built around a Moorish-style courtyard, where more intimate concerts are presented in the summer. During the winter, concerts are occasionally featured in the Music Room, an impressive, 70-foot-long room with a magnificent carved ceiling from an Italian palace and splendid tapestries. Guided tours (for a fee) are offered regularly Wednesday through Sunday and by appointment (you cannot visit the house on your own). Call 914-232-5035 for information on the tours and on the concerts.

After you have visited the house, take a stroll through the lovely formal gardens, especially in spring when they are most impressive. Picnic tables for the public are scattered around a pleasant apple orchard, and you can wander past a grape arbor, fountain, cedar walk, gazebo, or farther afield into the acres of woodlands that enclose the grounds.

20

A Riverfront Village Stroll and/or
a Mountain Climb Above
Cold Spring

HOW TO GET THERE:

*George Washington Bridge to Palisades Interstate Parkway north,
Bear Mountain Bridge, then Route 9D north along the river for
nine miles for a scenic route.*

*Alternate route: From Manhattan's east side: take the Major Dee-
gan to the New York Thruway to the Saw Mill River Parkway to
the Taconic. Exit at Route 301 west to Cold Spring.*

*From Manhattan's west side: Take the Henry Hudson Parkway,
which becomes the Saw Mill River Parkway, and follow the same
directions as above.*

The largely unspoiled Hudson River Valley remains one of our
favorite areas for walking. A leisurely stroll in Cold Spring, a
charming village on the east bank of the river across from West
Point and about 50 miles north of the city, followed by a scenic
climb up the Washburn Trail on nearby (less than a mile away)
Taurus Mountain, makes a fine excursion. The famed river views
from the village dock, as well as from the mountain summit, are
among the most spectacular in the Hudson Valley—especially in
fall, when the surrounding hills are in their full foliage splendor.

Cold Spring is the kind of place that takes the visitor back to
days of the horse and buggy and such riverfront traditions as
outdoor band concerts. The village is located in a scenic area that
has retained its character from the days of the first Dutch ex-
plorers. The vistas of the river are unobstructed by factories or
tall buildings. And Cold Spring's quaint Main Street is fun to amble
along, with its antique shops, a few very old houses, and the
remains of a foundry dock at river's edge.

The history of the village of Cold Spring begins well before
the Revolution. Its first settler was one Charles Davenport, who

arrived from England in 1729. Cold Spring is mentioned in history accounts when George Washington's army passed through the nearby Garrison Landing area on the day that Benedict Arnold's betrayal of the West Point fortifications was discovered. The encampment site of the army can be seen on a walking tour through the village, one of the several sites that date from the Revolutionary period. General Washington is thought to have given the place its name because he liked the cold spring water.

After the war, Cold Spring was chosen by President James Madison to be the site of one of four iron foundries to supply the government with munitions. By 1820 the foundry at the foot of Market Street was completed and turning out its first cannons, and Cold Spring was well on its way to prosperity. The first locomotive engines, including the DeWitt Clinton, were built here, as were the first Hudson River steamboats and the first iron water mains for New York City and Boston. Among other products manufactured were stoves, bells, steam engines, machinery, and the cast iron fronts of many buildings in the Soho section of Manhattan. Iron ore was brought to the foundry by river barge and then by train, and the town maintained its own fleet of sloops to carry finished products away. By mid-century it was the largest foundry in the country, producing munitions for the North in the Civil War. Employment in the foundry was as high as 1,400. In 1865 President Lincoln visited the foundry to thank the workers for their help in winning the war.

After the Civil War, Daniel Adams Butterfield, a Union major general who fought at Fredericksburg and Gettysburg among other battles, made his home, Cragside, in Cold Spring. This palatial house (which, unfortunately, burned down a few years ago) once welcomed the grand duchess of Russia and other dignitaries who arrived at the dock and were escorted there. The Butterfields were prominent citizens whose bequests gave the village a library and hospital, in the tradition of leading citizens of small towns across America. Another noteworthy citizen of Cold Spring was George Pope Morris, founder and editor of the *New York Mirror* and several other newspapers, as well as a popular-song composer. Among his guests, who also arrived by Hudson River steamboat, were many literary figures, including Charles Dickens.

By the middle of our century, preservationists realized that Cold Spring's main street deserved saving. The architecture of the area is still much as it was 100 years ago, and among the residents of the village are craftspeople and antique enthusiasts who want to keep it that way.

Who would like this walk? The village walk will appeal to most anyone and is easy and pleasant. The climb up the Washburn Trail is, on the other hand, fairly steep and recommended only for the fittest hikers. Of course, you can do one and not the other, depending on your energy, time, and inclination. Both parts of the outing will be enhanced if you take along a pair of binoculars and perhaps a camera. There are several cozy cafes, so you need not bring your own food unless you would prefer a picnic on the shore of the river. Do bring some water and/or a snack for the hike on the trail.

We think that fall is the best time to visit Cold Spring and its surroundings. The town by then has settled down after the bustle of the tourist season and, of course, the scenery is at its most glorious. However, if you like fireworks, you might want to come on the Fourth of July, when an impressive display can be viewed from the bandstand near the river. If your main interest is antiquing or shopping, remember that many antique shops are somewhat erratic in their hours and tend to be open only in the latter part of the week and weekend, especially during the off-season.

THE WALK

The more interesting shops and old houses are found on a steep three-block stretch of Main Street that runs down to the river bandstand across from Storm King Mountain. Lining the street are tiny shuttered frame buildings typical of 19th-century northern towns. From most merchants you can pick up a flier called "A Cold Spring Walking Tour," complete with map and all the major sites. Listed below are some of the places we encourage you to see. The Chapel of Our Lady, one of the most charming in the entire Hudson Valley, is reached by going down Main Street toward the river. Turn left just before the railroad tracks and then left again. The chapel looks out over the river. Since its completion in 1833, this small and simple but dignified building with its four Doric columns has often been painted and drawn.

The bandstand at the riverfront on West Street, the dock at the end of Market Street, the railroad station, and George Washington plaque, are all worth a look.

The Gouverneur Kemble Warren Home at 8 Fair Street is an

attractive Greek Revival building that can only be admired from
the outside. If you're interested (and if you're there on the right
day), stop by the Putnam County Historical Society Museum at 63
Chestnut Street. Here you'll see a portion of the original Foundry
School built in the 1820s to educate youngsters apprenticing at
the foundry. It is open to the public Wednesday from 9:30 A.M. to
4:00 P.M., Sunday from 2:00 to 5:00 P.M., and by appointment.
Phone: 914-265-2781.

The most charming (and popular) inn in the region, the Hudson
House, is worth a brief visit or meal, if time permits. Built in 1832
to house steamboat passengers, it has recently been tastefully
renovated. Its location, right on the river next to a small pier
where the steamboats docked, is special.

Of course we recommend you walk along the river to enjoy
the dramatic views. The Hudson is fairly narrow at this point and
you can clearly see the awe-inspiring and severe-looking Storm
King Mountain looming across the water, as well as West Point
farther down.

If you are a strong hiker and want to try the Washburn Trail,
drive back up Main Stret, turning left onto Route 9D. About .7
mile north is a clearing on the right, which will lead you to the
trail. You can park a few feet in from the road at the foot of a
driveway that used to lead to a now-abandoned stone quarry.
Walk, bearing left immediately (and following an unmarked path)
to a grassy slope and the first of the white blazes indicating the
beginning of the trail. You will see a trail register attached to a
tree. The Washburn Trail, 2.3 miles of fairly rough climbing, starts
from river level and goes 1,400 feet to the top of Mount Taurus.
As you ascend you'll see great views of Storm King and the river
valley to the west and south. After about two miles the trail meets
an old carriage road, which you'll stay on, past the summit of
Mount Taurus to get more wonderful panoramic views north and
west to Surprise Lake Valley, the Shawangunks, Breakneck Ridge,
and even the Catskills! This trail ends when it meets the Notch
Trail. You can either retrace your steps and go back down, or
continue on the Notch Trail to Dairy Road, which will lead you
back to Route 9D, about .25 mile north from where you started.

AFTER THE WALK

The surroundings of Cold Spring offer several sites that are worth a visit.

Garrison's Landing is a tiny settlement with an impeccable 19th-century train station on the banks of the river. Its old-fashioned charm and unspoiled architecture made it the choice for the setting of the movie *Hello, Dolly!*, in the 1960s. Don't miss St. Philips Church in the Highlands on Route 9D, a simple stone church with pitched slate roof built in the 1840s, and St. Joseph's Catholic chapel, also a quaint building. Garrison's Landing is the site of many pottery studios and the Garrison Art Center displays some of these crafts. You can call them at 914-424-3960, or take your chances and visit uninvited.

While in the area, visit Boscobel off Route 9D, a classical 1804 mansion built in the Federal style and beautifully preserved. You are invited to stroll through its lovely gardens and orangeries overlooking the Hudson. Inside there are rooms filled with antiques. Call 914-265-3638 for information.

Nearby and also on Route 9D is Dick's (Dix) Castle, a typical eccentric's folly and giant Moorish style curiosity modeled after the Alhambra in Spain.

Pollepel Island, a historic island which can be seen from Route 9D north of Cold Spring, contains the ruins of a Scottish-style castle built at the turn of the century. There is no access to the island now except by private boat, but it adds an exotic touch to the landscape.

21

A Reflective Lakeside Walk . . .
Only One Half Hour from the City
Rockefeller State Park Preserve, Tarrytown

HOW TO GET THERE:
Take the Major Deegan north to the New York State Thruway to exit 9 to Route 9 northbound, through the villages of Tarrytown and North Tarrytown. Turn right on Route 117 and follow signs for the preserve. Entrance to the park is on the right.

This is a country walk surprisingly close to the city. The mixture of meadows, lake and wooded paths (with occasional horseback riders appearing on the bridle paths) gives the walker the feeling of being on an English country estate. The grounds and paths are well tended, but not overdone, the natural beauty of a Hudson Valley landscape unspoiled, the lake clean and rippling. The Preserve is indeed that—preserved for walking and enjoying the weather and feeding the ducks or observing nature. Despite its proximity to a bustling village and busy highways, once inside the preserve you'll find it hard to believe these 750 acres are not a hundred miles from civilization. The park was given by the Rockefeller family estate to the public just a few years ago, and apparently not many people know about it, for it is wonderfully uncrowded. There are some 14 miles of carriage and walking paths, and the beautiful little Swan Lake covers 24 acres. There is a variety of terrains, including riverside lanes—the winding Pocantico River makes its way through the park—wetlands, woods, fields, and the path around the lake. Outdoor enthusiasts who use the preserve include birders, photographers, cross-country skiers, and artists, as well as horseback riders. The park asks its visitors not to disturb or collect anything. There is no picnicking, but you can take trail lunches to designated areas. Also forbidden are radios, unleashed pets, smoking, motorized vehicles, alcoholic beverages, and camping and swimming. These rules do not seem excessive, for the stillness and cleanliness of the grounds are a wonderful antidote to the bustle of life outside. It is an ideal place for reflection as well as energetic walking. The lakeside, in particular, is an oasis of quiet beauty, where you can watch the expanding ripples of water as a duck swims by.

This is an ideal walk for families, including elderly walkers or children. Most of the trails (all color marked) are not difficult and your walk can be as long as you wish to make it, for a good map (available at the entrance in a box on the side of the shed) will allow you to crisscross and combine one trail with another. Take good walking shoes, binoculars, some bread for the ducks if you wish, and perhaps a sketchbook or camera. A number of the trails are listed as steep grades; these provide wonderful upward climbs that will take you to spots from which you will get a panoramic view of the Hudson below. The map at the shed lists the difficulty and length of each trail, so be sure to read it before you set out. One of the trails will take you along the Old Croton Aqueduct Trail (see walk 17) which runs all the way from Croton to the city. In fact, if you are an adventurous walker—in addition to a strong and energetic one—you can start out at Croton and walk south through woodland and village, through this preserve, and on to 173rd Street in Manhattan. (To take that walk you should pick up the Croton Aqueduct walk directory from: the New York State Parks, Taconic Region, Staatsburg, N.Y. 12580, or call 914-889-4100.)

We recommend this walk in any season, including winter and in snowy weather. Those walkers who enjoy a winter hike can't find a better one than this: parking is easy, the terrain is mostly level, and there are no snowmobiles or other noisy intrusions. Winter birds enjoy the lake and woods. In fall the foliage is glorious and its reflection in the still lake waters lovely to look at. Summer and spring are, of course, perfect times to visit, so this is indeed a year-round site for walkers.

THE WALK

After leaving your car at the entrance parking area (free), you can choose which trail to take. You'll begin at the parking area. The Swan Lake Trail, a real strolling path, will take you along the edges of the lake and onto Ridge Trail, where you can see the lake from above on a hillside, or onto Ash Tree and Overlook trails. Both are steep paths with panoramic views of the lake. If you start from the parking area on Nature's Way Trail, you'll see some nice rocky areas in a lovely wooded setting. That route can lead you to the old Colonial road called Old Sleepy Hollow Trail, a gently sloping roadway. If you continue on that trail and turn left at the fork, you'll come to the Pocantico River, which ripples alongside the path. If you choose the opposite direction you will find Eagle Hill Trail, a steep climb with a great view of the Hudson as a reward for your efforts. These are only a few of the 20 different trails identified by the park. We suggest a plan before you start off: add up the mileage in advance so that you know just how much you can manage and still return in one piece to your car.

AFTER THE WALK

The location of this preserve is conveniently close to several tourist attractions. The historic region of Tarrytown (the Sleepy

Hollow of earlier times) includes several historic restorations, fine antique homes, Sleepy Hollow Cemetery where Washington Irving is buried, and the wonderful Pocantico Union Church with its Chagall windows. All of these attractions are described at the end of walk 18. You can visit any of them after your outing, or you might want to combine this walk with the exploration of Sleepy Hollow Cemetery itself (walk 18).

THE HUDSON VALLEY (WEST)

22

An Autumn Walk in the Footsteps
of the Hudson River Artists
Kaaterskill Falls

HOW TO GET THERE:

George Washington Bridge to Palisades Parkway to the New York State Thruway north, exit at Saugerties (exit 20). Take Route 32 to Palenville, and Route 23A toward Haines Falls. After about 3.5 miles you'll see a small sign on the right-hand side of the road indicating the way to Kaaterskill Falls (you will also see a gorge and another waterfall). Go another .25 mile until you reach a parking area on the left side of the road. Walk down to the sign indicating the falls.

When American painters celebrated the glories of our landscape more than a century ago, it was the Hudson River Valley and the Catskill Mountain region that inspired them. The rushing waterfalls, jagged rocks and cliffs, and beautiful trees of the region became the subject for dozens of paintings, many of them as beloved (or more) today as when they first appeared.

Happily, that landscape still exists, much of it unspoiled and protected; in fact, some areas have an entirely new growth of forest. The Hudson River artists would be elated (as we were) to discover the same breathtaking lookouts and rugged forest paths.

We decided to follow the footsteps of a number of them in the Kaaterskill Falls region that they immortalized. Our walk was probably more difficult than theirs (notwithstanding paint box, sketchbook, and easel in tow), since conservation efforts have closed some trails, and the train and convenient horse and buggy routes have been discontinued. In the 19th century, during the heyday of the grand Catskill hotels, guests would arrive by train, get off near the head of the Falls, and walk down a short distance to view them. However, we persevered on foot, and it was well worth it!

There are three particularly spectacular parts of the Kaaterskill walk. One, of course, is the falls, a magical hidden spot that looks quite the same as when painted by Thomas Cole, the "father" of the Hudson River School. The falls, with the two-part cascade over the rosy stone mountainside, were painted three times by Cole, as well as by other artists, making them one of the most famous 19th-century landscape subjects of all. If before or after your visit you would like to see how Kaaterskill Falls looked to the artists, there are several books on the Hudson River School with fine reproductions. You'll find Cole's drawings of them (at the Detroit Institute of Arts), and three paintings (one of which is in Tuscaloosa, Alabama, at the Warner Collection). You'll also find one by Sanford Gifford, a Hudson River painter of the next generation, at the Metropolitan Museum. Later, Winslow Homer and Currier & Ives created their own versions of the falls.

Many of the artists stayed at the most famous hotel of the period—the Mountain House—a columned and elegant hostelry set literally on the edge of one of the great cliffs and overviews of the Hudson Valley, another dramatic spot. We climbed to the very

site of the inn (no longer there, alas) and stared out at the ribbon
of the Hudson in the distance and the spectacular scenery below
us. Our third scenic location is reached by taking the trail (see
below for details) from the site of the hotel along the cliff toward
a wonderful rocky plateau appropriately called Artist Rock. We
could imagine the painters' excitement at a vista almost too beautiful to paint. Along the way to Artist Rock we passed several sites,
quite overgrown now, from which they could see the great hotel
in the distance. Jasper Cropsey painted it (Minneapolis Museum
of Art), Cole drew it (Brooklyn Museum), and Sanford Gifford
painted it in autumn glory (Trinity College, Hartford). Unfortunately, the hotel's rates became too steep for the artists, many of
whom bought homes in the area instead and continued to paint
the region around it anyway.

The entire scenic region lies along Kaaterskill Creek that makes
its way between rolling mountains quite close to the Hudson. As
you drive there you'll take a winding mountain road (known as
Rip Van Winkle Trail) through a third oft-painted spot, Kaaterskill
Clove. ("Clove," widely used in this Dutch-settled region, is a
ravine or mountain gully, after the Dutch for cleft.) Kaaterskill
Clove (pictured by Asher Durand in the probably most famous
Hudson Valley painting of all, "Kindred Spirits," now in the New
York Public Library) is a scenic convergence of glorious trees,
craggy mountains, gorges, a narrow serpentine river, and jutting
rocks. Kaaterskill Clove was painted so often that there must have
been artists at every turn! Among the most famous works are one
by Durand called "Kaaterskill Clove" (belonging to the private
Century Association of N.Y.C.); Cole's "The Clove, Catskills" (at
the New Britain Museum of Art, New Britain, Connecticut); and
"Kauterskill Clove," by Sanford Gifford (at the Metropolitan Museum in New York). But these are only a few of the works of the
same subject.

You will enjoy searching out these and other works and tracking
their locations in this area. Some of the sites are now unreachable:
for example, about .25 mile of the Escarpment Trail that the artists
and others once took from the Mountain House across the mountain to the top of the falls is no longer open to walkers, who now
must climb up from the bottom. However, the exact spot where

each artist set up to view the clove, or the many unspecific views of woods and mountains (which we know were made in the neighborhood) would be a fine research project for a hardy walker, reproductions in hand.

We settled for the three most famous locales and were well rewarded for our hikes through some rough terrain. The description below will give you an idea of how to go about tracking the artists of our past.

This walk, being one of our more rugged ventures, is recommended for those who are in relatively good physical condition. Be sure to wear sturdy shoes and bring drinking water along! The best time to go is during the fall, at the peak of foliage. Summers tend to be crowded with campers and hikers; the snowy and icy paths become too arduous in winter; and the going is too wet in spring. Try to go on a weekday, if possible, as weekends are busy with walkers in summer and fall.

THE WALK

For this three-part walk:

Park your car at the public parking area on Route 23A, about 3.5 miles after leaving Palenville and Route 32. Walk downhill about .25 mile to a small bridge overlooking Kaaterskill Creek and Bastion Falls, which are quite grand in themselves. You will see a smallish sign indicating Kaaterskill Falls to be .5 mile up from there (it seemed longer to us). On the other side of the road is a wonderful view of Kaaterskill Clove, perhaps one of the same views admired and painted by the Hudson River artists.

Walk uphill, following the rather sporadic yellow trail markers, which lead you more or less parallel to the creek all the way to the falls. (If you lose sight of the trail markers, which is likely, keep walking next to the creek and you won't get lost.) The going is quite arduous, as the "path" (which is hardly one at all) has been eroded and footing is uneven. You clamber over large rocks, twisted tree roots, decaying branches, and leaves, which can be slippery. Even though the distance is fairly short, the trek will be difficult for those who are not in fairly good physical condition. (We saw some poor souls trying to negotiate their climb on all fours!) But your efforts are well rewarded. The forest is dense with hemlocks and many deciduous trees that illuminate it with bright colors in the fall. As you make the rugged but exhilarating climb up you feel somewhat like an explorer in a primeval forest. Finally, you reach a large boulder in the middle of the creek bed from where you get a full front view of the falls in all their splendor. And what majestic falls they are! At 260 feet, they are the highest in New York State (including Niagara Falls which, however, are much broader, of course). The two slender and elegant cascades are divided by a rock basin and surrounded by a landscape that is wild, rugged, and uncorrupted—truly a quintessential romantic scene. After you have stopped long enough to rest and take in this marvelous site, you must retrace your steps, since you can no longer proceed up alongside the falls for a side view.

As we descended the hill, we felt elated and ready to see more. If you feel the same way, drive up to the North Lake State Campsite, a park from which you can walk to the site where the Mountain House once stood, only a few miles away. To reach the park from Route 23A, continue in the same direction to Haines Falls and take a right on Route 18, following signs for the North Lake State Campsite. You arrive at an efficient-looking toll booth where you pay a small fee and are given a map and trail guide that shows you (more or less) how to find the Mountain House site. You have now entered Catskill State Park, a woodsy region popular with campers and hikers and filled with clearly marked trails. Park at North Lake, where the road comes to an end. You'll see a small sandy beach, picnic and rest room facilities, and signs telling you what is prohibited (just about everything except hiking). To reach the Mountain House site, follow the signs up a gentle hill until you come to the commemorative marker for the hotel. Continue toward the escarpment for what has been—and continues to be— regarded as one of the most impressive and vast panoramas in the East. The landscape seems to go on forever: miles of the glistening Hudson are laid out in front of you, surrounded by the lush river valley. Beyond you can see the Taconic and Berkshire ranges.

After gazing at this remarkable view for some time, we ventured forth, map in hand, toward Artist Rock (about .5 mile away, on the Escarpment Trail), to see if we could find a good view of the Catskill Mountain House site. Follow the signs for Artist Rock, Sunset Rock, and Newmans Ledge, trails all quite clearly marked with blue blazes. Once you are past picnic areas and other indications of organized parkland, you find yourself on virgin, somewhat hilly terrain along the cliffs, from where you have one extraordinary view after another, including several from which the Mountain House site could have been seen. After a short but arduous climb on top of large boulders (but, fortunately, not near the edge of the cliff!), you reach a plateau which appears almost to be (but isn't) a man-made terrace, so regular is the rock surface. Continue until you come to what is unmistakably Artist Rock, another great lookout point over a ledge. Now the trees around it are overgrown, making it difficult to see the Catskill Mountain House site; but you can imagine that this may have been a particularly dramatic vista some 100 years ago. If you wish, continue on to Sunset Rock and Newmans Ledge.

If you are still able and adventuresome, go back to the hotel site and set out on the other section of the Escarpment Trail. It used to be possible to reach the falls from above, along a network of trails that still exist. This extensive trail system includes miles of fabulous views atop tall cliffs overlooking the Hudson River Valley and Kaaterskill Clove. The hike from the Catskill Mountain House site to the falls is about four miles, but the trail along the ledges is difficult and dangerous, and the section of it that actually goes to the falls was recently definitively closed as unsafe. So your walk will not reach the falls from above. Still, you will not be disappointed, for the part you can still do is spectacular.

AFTER THE WALK

While in a Hudson River artist's frame of mind, you might want to take a detour and visit Olana, the home of Frederick Church, one of the more flamboyant (and also more successful) exponents of that school. Built in 1874, this eclectic and eccentric house is a sort of Moorish/Victorian creation filled to the brim with furnishings and bric-a-brac that Church collected in his world travels.

Aside from its more "kitschy" aspects, it does house some very fine paintings by Church and other Hudson River artists and is an amusing place to visit. The view from the house (perched 500 feet above the Hudson) and its 250-acre park is special. The park is open to the public for boating, picnicking, and nature walks; the house is open from May to October, Wednesday through Saturday 9:00 A.M. to 5:00 P.M., Sundays 1:00 to 5:00 P.M. Phone: 518-828-0135. Olana is about five miles south of the city of Hudson on the east side of the Hudson River. To get there from Kaaterskill Falls retrace your steps and get back on to the New York State Thruway, go north and exit at Catskill (exit 21), where you can cross the river. Take Route 9G north for a few miles and follow the signs.

23

An Off-Season Lake Walk
Rockland Lake, Congers

HOW TO GET THERE:

From west side of Manhattan: West Side Highway, George Washington Bridge, Palisades Parkway, exit 4, north on Route 9W. Go about 9 miles on Route 9W. Access to Rockland State Park is off Route 9W and is well marked, and there are several parking areas. From east side of Manhattan: FDR Drive, Harlem River Drive, George Washington Bridge, and follow same directions as above.

The Rockland Lake walk is a pleasant circular three-mile jaunt along the edge of the water. The lake lies within Rockland Lake State Park, 588 acres of somewhat developed parklands with sports and picnic facilities. During busy summer weekends the park is crowded and noisy with the sounds of blaring radios. For this reason we recommend this walk off-season or on weekdays, when it is wonderfully peaceful. This is a flat, easy walk that will appeal to joggers, bikers, and nature lovers.

Rockland Lake is a post-glacial lake, once famous for the excellent quality of the ice produced here before refrigeration. In fact, its ice was exported not only to nearby areas, but also as far away as the Caribbean. The remnants of ice houses used to store the ice can still be seen in the park.

Although you are never really far away from "civilization," this lakeside walk is still bucolic. Willows line the path; there are peaceful views of fishermen in rowboats, surrounded by water lilies. There are ducks, swans, and geese everywhere, encouraged by families with children who bring food for them. In the fall you might see mute swans, originally domesticated birds from Europe, that live in pairs and sometimes reach the age of 100.

Avoid the weekends of July and August! Otherwise, this is an all-season walk. If you plan to do more than walk—you can fish, ice skate, row a boat, or watch for birds—you should check to see when those activities are available. (Call 914-786-2701 for

N

W · E

S

P

NATURE
CENTER

WALKING TRAIL

FISHING
AREA

TO LAKE
RD →
and
LANDING RD.
and HOOK MT.
RIVER TRAIL

~ ROCKLAND
LAKE ~ ~

P

ROUTE 9W

P

An OFF-SEASON
LAKE WALK ~

TO NYACK
and N.Y.C.

general information.) Birders should go between March and October; there is good ice skating and ice fishing on cold winter days; and you can rent a rowboat, rain or shine, from March to the end of October. Winter is especially nice if there's not a cold wind blowing.

This is an outing for people of any age or physical ability. The less energetic will enjoy ambling along this mostly shaded path at a leisurely pace; children will like feeding the waterfowl; nature lovers can look for various species of flora and fauna. Others might just like to be in a quiet setting with pleasant views at every turn.

If you are a birder, bring binoculars. Bring along a picnic; there are several lakeside picnic tables, but you will also find plenty of shade trees to sit under or lookout points from which to enjoy the view.

THE WALK

Park either near the swimming pool and bathhouse (for a small fee) or by the fishing and comfort station where parking is free. You can't miss the path: in addition to being a footpath, it is a bike trail and marked as such. It doesn't matter in which direction you start, or at what point you begin your walk, as you will eventually come back to your starting point.

Take in your surroundings: the many wonderful wildflowers and shrubs that bloom along the path during June, the trees reflected in the lake, and the sounds of birds overhead. You might be able to identify some of the following species: downy woodpecker, song sparrow, red-winged blackbird, tree swallow, mockingbird, yellow warbler, Baltimore oriole, gold finch, catbird, and swamp sparrow.

Eventually you will come to the nature center, a smallish wooden structure at the north side of the lake. There you can see displays of live snakes, toads, frogs, fish, and salamanders indigenous to these parts. From the nature center there are two marshy trails (totaling about .5 mile) which take you through a woodland swamp. You walk atop a boardwalk through dark woods, past a variety of plants that are identified on markers. You'll see spicebush (early settlers made tea from its fragrant twigs and leaves), red maples, white ash, red oak, tulip trees, swamp loosestrife, ferns, and red osiers. It is a pleasant surprise to come upon a clearing and good view of the lake, from where the second trail begins. This lakeside bog trail, a shaded leafy walk with a canopy of shrubs overhead, takes you past wild flowering bushes, swamp azaleas, arrowwood (used by Indians for arrow shafts), high-bush blueberry, and winterberry. There is a lovely second lookout point where you might want to pause briefly to enjoy the scenery. The path leads back to the main lakeside walk, where you can continue, if you like.

AFTER THE WALK

You might want to take advantage of the other activities Rockland Lake can provide. There is excellent fishing in both winter and summer. Licenses, available at local sporting goods stores, are required. Since 1980, the lake has been stocked with hybrid muskellunge, chain pickerel, bass, perch, and sunfish. You can rent a rowboat and tackle from March through October, seven days a week, regardless of the weather. Call 914-268-3888 for information.

24

Walking Through a Sculpturescape
Storm King Art Center, Mountainville

HOW TO GET THERE:
George Washington Bridge to Palisades Parkway north, to New York State Thruway. Take exit 16 (Harriman) to Route 32 north. Go about 10 miles on Route 32. Follow signs to Storm King Art Center (first left after a small bridge, onto Orrs Mill Road, then another left onto Old Pleasant Hill Road). For information, call 914-534-3115 or 534-3190.

You're driving on winding roads through the rolling countryside in the Hudson Valley. Suddenly you find yourself in front of an extraordinary place where large, brilliant, imposing structures reach up to the sky in a startling contrast to the environment. You are at the Storm King Art Center, probably the most impressive and important outdoor sculpture park and museum in the United States. It would be hard to imagine a place where works of art are more dramatically displayed. Located 55 miles north of New York City in a valley between Storm King and Schunemunk Mountain, it encompasses a large collection of more than 200 modern sculptures, many of massive proportions. They are set in an expansive landscape of grassy hills and vast fields, surrounded by acres of woodland. Walking through the spacious grounds (some 400 acres) and seeing these giant abstract sculptures perched atop hills and spread out in valleys below is an inspiring, if startling, visual experience. Mostly made of metal and stone in massive geometric forms, these sculptures tower like stark visitors from another world. We can think of no real equivalent to Storm King Art Center. While there are other sculpture gardens in America and Europe, they are smaller in scale and more urban in setting. There is something quintessentially American about the combination of space and contemporary art.

The center, founded in 1960, occupies the grounds of what was formerly the residence of one Vermont Hatch. His elegant

Normandy-style chateau, built in 1935 with the stones from a nearby Hudson River mansion destined for demolition, is now used to display traveling sculpture exhibits, as well as some of the more delicate pieces of the permanent collection. Hatch's great friend and neighbor, Ted Ogden (a businessman, farmer, world traveler, and art collector), gradually converted this wonderful estate into a sculpture museum, after having been inspired by some photographs showing Henry Moore sculptures on a sheep ranch in Scotland. In a major coup, he acquired 14 pieces

111

of sculpture by the late David Smith at one time, generating a great deal of interest for the museum. To this group he added important works by such contemporary sculptors as Alexander Calder, Anthony Caro, Mark di Suvero, Charles Ginnever, Robert Grosvenor, Barbara Hepworth, Henry Moore, David Von Schlegell, and Isaac Witkin, to name a few. Since Ogden's death in 1974, more sculptures have found their permanent home at Storm King. As they are added, more land is cleared, hills are created or altered to accommodate them, and new paths are built. The landscape of Storm King is ever changing.

One of the wonderful things here is that you can go right up to the sculptures—if you have the stamina to cover the necessary distances—or you can view them from afar. You can take a one-hour guided walking tour for a fee, Wednesday through Sunday from May 1 to November 20. (Reservations are required; call 914-534-3190.) However, we think that it's more fun to roam on your own throughout this vast place and to see whatever appeals to you. You can walk for miles up and down the various hills, or you can limit yourself to the particular areas that interest you. (At the entrance you'll find a map that shows you where to find what.)

This walk can be as leisurely or as arduous as you make it, depending on what you want to cover. It's a walk that most people would enjoy; of course art lovers will find it most stimulating, but so will many others—particularly foreign visitors—who will be intrigued by this unique environment. Children will find it great fun to traipse up and down hills, past structures like none they may have ever seen before. Although there are some signs requesting specifically that you not touch a particular work, others have no such restrictions. In fact, an impressive work by Isamu Noguchi, "Momo Taro," has been partially hollowed out so that the visitor can actually sit inside it!

When you go to Storm King you should take a picnic, as there are tables in grassy areas near the lower parking lot (and few restaurants in the vicinity). The center is open daily, except Tuesdays, from April 1 to November 30, from noon to 5:30 P.M. (In winter, when the museum is closed, the smaller, more delicate sculptures are taken inside; others are wrapped up like suburban shrubbery; and the hardier are left outside as they are, to brave the elements.) Because of the spaciousness of the grounds, you never have the impression of crowds—outside anyway. Of course, the inside museum—with its limited space—is likely to be busy on weekends.

THE WALK

After parking your car, proceed to the main house, which is the museum's entrance and center. There you pay a small fee and pick up whatever literature you wish, including a guide to the museum. Start off in the immediate vicinity of the house, where the smaller, more intimate sculptures are displayed. Close to the entrance is a fine piece by Louise Nevelson, which you should not miss, as well as some more representational works by such artists as Emilio Greco, Jo Davidson, and Henri Etienne-Martin, placed around the house amid formal gardens. Nearby you will see a group of Ionic columns, which look like sculptures themselves. We were told they come from the original estate that provided some of the building material for the house. The columns look perfect in this setting, adding a touch of romanticism to the scene. On the other side of the house you come to a group of David Smith sculptures, which invariably attract the largest number of visitors. (Only eight of the 13 Smith sculptures are displayed outside; the others, which are more delicate, can be seen indoors.)

As you go beyond the more formal garden space next to the house, the landscape becomes freer and more open, as well as more hilly. An intermediate (in size) group of works by such sculptors as Henry Moore and Alexander Calder are within the middle distance from the house. As you go farther from the house, the works become larger and more commanding. Noguchi's "Momo Taro" is dramatically placed on a knoll overlooking a valley. The massive pieces by Alexander Liberman ("Ascent," "Eve," "Adonai") are on the outer edges of the cleared grounds; Tal Streeter's bright orange "Endless Column" zigzags its way up to the sky, towering over trees; Mark di Suvero's gigantic works are in a distant valley below the house and a walk to view them up close is quite a trek. Walking through this incredible landscape stimulates thought on the nature of art and the function of art in nature. Are these works in harmony with their natural environment or are they an imposition on it? Does the place work as a setting for such art? No matter what conclusions you draw, we are sure that you will not be disappointed in your outing at Storm King.

AFTER THE WALK

You might want to take a look at West Point Military Academy, since it's so close. To get to West Point, follow scenic Route 218 through the village of Cornwall, going south for a few miles. Roads are clearly marked. Stop at the visitors' center at the entrance and pick up a map for a self-guided walking or driving tour. We suggest you drive around the sprawling campus—which resembles a fortified castle, with crenellated towers—before you park, to get oriented. There are lovely views of the Hudson at every turn. Points of interest include: Academy Chapel, with its Gothic-style features, brick and stone interior arches, high vaulted ceilings, and stained glass windows; the Thayer Museum, across campus; and Trophy Point, overlooking the river, where links of iron chains were used to prevent British ships from coming up the river during the Revolutionary War. (See walk 26 for the origin of the iron.) But the most fun is to view the marching cadets in their familiar uniforms. If you go on a weekend, especially in fall (when there might be a football game), be prepared for the inevitable crowds. West Point is open daily from 9:00 A.M. to 4:30 P.M., and there is no admission charge.

25

Along a Railroad Track and Back
by the Hudson
Piermont

HOW TO GET THERE:

From Manhattan's west side: West Side Highway, George Washington Bridge, Palisades Interstate Parkway. Get off at exit 4, go north on Route 9W. After about 3.3 miles (you will pass a bridge and two sets of traffic lights) there is a sharp right hand turn off of Route 9W (Ash Street in Piermont). The sign reads "Piermont Business District." Go down a steep hill to the center of the village. From Manhattan's east side: FDR Drive, George Washington Bridge, and follow same directions as above.

From your childhood you may remember walking along a railroad track, including the frightening moment when you walked across the wooden trestle. An abandoned track through rural country side evokes a bygone era of America.

In Piermont, only 17 miles from New York City, you can amble along a former railroad track bed—called the Erie Path—high above the Hudson, overlooking the Victorian frame houses that line the river. Coming back, we suggest you go down to River Road and enjoy the river and the houses up close. This walk is mostly flat, except for where you descend to river level and return to railroad track level to pick up your car. What is surprising is how solitary this path is, except for an occasional jogger or birdwatcher.

The tracks here were originally built by the Erie Railroad, the first long distance railroad in the U.S., connecting two ports— Piermont (as its easternmost point) to Dunkirk, New York, on the shores of Lake Erie—some 450 miles to the west. The railroad was formally inaugurated in Piermont on May 14, 1851, amid great pomp with many illustrious guests, including President Millard Fillmore and his secretary of state, Daniel Webster. Thousands of people lined the streets to catch a glimpse of the event. Several dignitaries then took the train to Dunkirk, where another huge celebration around a 300-foot dining table awaited them.

Piermont and the other towns along the route all prospered as a result of the railroad, but these boom years were short. By

1861 the railroad's major commercial traffic went to New Jersey destinations rather than to the Hudson Valley, and this section of the road was used for commuter traffic only (by then many city dwellers had already become exurbanites). This commuter rail line, called the North Branch, operated from Nyack to Jersey City until the 1960s, when it was abandoned. In 1975 it was designated a park and has been enjoyed by walkers, joggers, and even occasional horseback riders ever since.

This is a leafy, shady walk in spring and fall, and a sparkling, dramatic walk in winter. It's often very hot and humid in summer. It is not an arduous hike and is mostly flat, but it does include some hills. The distance varies, depending on where you leave your car. At its shortest and flattest it's a two mile walk round trip (if you never go down to the river). We recommend this walk for fairly energetic people who appreciate nature, views, and looking at Victorian houses.

This outing requires good walking shoes, insect repellent (in summer), and water. While you can picnic along the wooded trail, there are no places to stop for a picnic along River Road; this is an area of private homes. Piermont offers one very pleasant eating place—"The Turning Point"—and other small, informal spots.

THE WALK

You have two options, depending on how energetic you feel and how much time you have:

For a five mile round trip walk, drive back to Sparkill (south) via Piermont's River Road (Piermont Avenue) alongside the creek. When you reach the railroad tracks in Sparkill, park your car near the crossing. You'll find a small dirt path, which marks the beginning of the Erie Path. As you walk on this pleasant woodland way above the villages of Sparkill and Piermont, notice the wide variety of trees around you: tulip, beech, oak, ash, birch, mulberry, locust, and dogwood.

Although heavily wooded, the trail has occasional clearings with expanses of wild honeysuckle, mock orange, wild roses, smartweed, dayflowers, wild grapevines, and raspberries. You'll find birds, rabbits, and other small creatures as well along this trail.

After about one mile you'll come to a brief interruption in the path, where a paved road (Ash Street) cuts across, but continue straight ahead on the Erie Path past the old station (now a private house). After another mile or so you'll reach a trestle, which overlooks a dramatic ravine, where you might like to stop and take in the view. This is especially scenic in winter when you have excellent visibility of the gorge. After about .5 mile you'll come to a fence across the road, which you can go around easily. Look for a small path to the right just beyond. This is Station Lane (unmarked as such), which cuts rather precipitously down the hill and eventually connects with River Road along the Hudson. Station Lane is for those who are sure of foot. Watch for poison ivy!

When you reach River Road, turn right and proceed south, along this charming winding road past the Victorian houses. You will come to the center of the village of Piermont after about 1.5 miles. Find your way back to your car, following the road along Sparkill Creek.

If you decide that a five mile walk is too much, try a shorter version of not more than 3.5 miles. We suggest you park near the Piermont library (off Ash Street) and find the Erie Path nearby. For an even shorter walk, do just a portion of the Erie Path and simply retrace your steps. You can always drive past the old houses on River Road.

AFTER THE WALK

Tallman Mountain State Park, contiguous to Piermont, can be reached by foot from a dirt road next to the Piermont marsh or by car from Rockland Road right off Route 9W. It is well worth a detour. There are playing fields for various sports, a large swimming pool (next to the river), tennis courts, scenic trails for jogging, cross-country skiing, and biking (follow green signs for the bike route), and picnic grounds overlooking the Hudson.

The historic town of Tappan, a couple of miles south and west of Piermont, is an authentic and unspoiled village originally settled by the Dutch in the 17th century. Here you can walk through the historic district in a relatively short time and visit some of the old houses and monuments:

Start with the DeWint House (where you can pick up a handout describing the various historic sites). Built in 1700, this is the oldest house in Rockland County. George Washington used this house as his army headquarters on several occasions during the Revolutionary War and it was here that he condemned Major John André to death for being a spy. The old stone-and-brick cottage with green shutters is surrounded by pleasantly shaded grounds, old-fashioned flower gardens, and tall stately trees (copper beech, Norway spruces, magnolias, locusts, white pines, Chinese elms, maples, and Canadian hemlocks). An immense weeping willow, said to be the largest of its kind in the country, stands next to the carriage house.

Near the DeWint House you'll find the Tappan library, dating from 1750, with its authentic Colonial garden.

Just down the road you'll come to the Yoast Mabie Tavern, known as the '76 House (now a restaurant), where Major André was imprisoned.

On the village green you'll see the Reformed Church of Tappan, originally built in the late 17th century and then rebuilt in the 19th. Next to it are the old burying grounds, where you can wander around past old gravesites. Opposite the green stands the Manse, built in 1724 and in continuous use since then.

26

Hiking on an Old Iron Mine Trail in the Ramapo Hills
Harriman State Park

HOW TO GET THERE:

George Washington Bridge to Palisades Interstate Parkway north. Follow signs for Route 6 west. Almost immediately you will come to a traffic circle. Go around most of the circle and take Seven Lakes Drive. After about four miles you will come to two lakes on either side of the road. The parking area you want is to your right, next to Lake Skannatati.

This three mile circular hike combines an interesting bit of history with a beautiful natural setting. Harriman State Park in the Ramapo Hills is filled with historic sites, among them a great many 19th-century iron mines. In this region iron mining, which began in the mid-18th century, had become an important industry by the time of the Revolutionary War, when about 14 percent of the entire world's supply of iron ore was produced here. The area was not only endowed with massive supplies of the mineral; but the plentiful waterways for powering furnaces and large forests for making the needed charcoal made it a perfect place for iron production. Some of its present-day scenic and recreational lakes were once ponds and streams that were dammed for water supplies. By the mid-19th century mines and blast furnaces proliferated, including the Arden Furnace, now called Clove Iron Furnace (see below). For those who worked in the mines (mostly Irish immigrants, including boys as young as 11), conditions were harsh at best. The work was arduous, winters rugged, and disease rampant. Many died of malaria or black fly disease spread by mosquitoes from nearby swamps. And the land was ravaged: masses of trees were cut down and mines were blasted continually. It's hard to imagine that what is now a truly peaceful stretch of forests and lakes was, only 100 years ago, a smoldering and denuded wasteland.

The mines in the region were abandoned in the late 1880s, when iron mining proved more profitable and efficient near the anthracite coal beds of Pennsylvania. The Harriman family bought many thousands of acres in the Ramapo region at auction, and gradually—from the early 1900s on—gave up large parcels to be used for public parkland.

Today, 80-square-mile Harriman State Park provides the walker, hiker, and naturalist with a wonderful variety of trails in a vast, unusually scenic environment of mountains, streams, forests, and (man-made) pristine lakes. Because the terrain is hilly with some fairly strenuous climbing and uneven footing, the walk is recommended for those who are used to rougher hikes.

The excursion we recommend includes only a few of the numerous iron mines, but enough to give you an idea of what they were like. They vary in depth from a few feet to hundreds, even thousands, of feet. Some are like caves that you can actually enter;

others are simply holes in the ground. That so many have survived erosion is probably due to the fact that wood beams and retaining walls were often built around them to prevent their caving in.

This hike is one that will appeal to families with children, as well as to fit walkers. Children will love the adventuresome aspect of discovering the mines as they go along. However, they should be cautioned to be careful, as many of the mines are not sealed. It might be fun to take along a magnet to test rocks next to the mines for iron ore content. (This method, in fact, was one of several used to determine where to locate mines. Another was to look for rocks that appeared rusty.)

If you are interested, you might also want to take a plumb line, to test the depth of the mines you pass along the way. In addition, we suggest you use a trail map of Harriman State Park, even though the trails are clearly marked. (You can get one either by mail from the New York-New Jersey Trail Conference, P.O. Box 2250, New York, NY 10116, or by visiting the central office at Bear Mountain State Park, next to Harriman.) There are wonderful spots for picnics atop large boulders, or in shaded glades of evergreens, or overlooking a lake. Wear hiking clothes, especially sturdy hiking boots.

This is a walk for all seasons and all days of the week. The area is vast, so that you are never overwhelmed by crowds, even at busy times of the year. We especially enjoyed this hike in fall, because of the incredible colors of nature, and in winter, when the tracks of the deer and other animals could be seen in the pristine snow.

THE WALK

Leave your car at the parking area for boating and fishing next to Lake Skannatati (Lake Askoti is across the road). There are two trails that begin at the northern corner of the parking area. Take the so-called Arden-Surebridge Trail, marked by a white blaze with red dots. You will begin a somewhat strenuous climb up Pine Swamp Mountain; at the summit are some spectacular glacial boulders. You will come to a lovely lookout point to view serene Lake Skannatati below. Continue on the path, which meanders up and down hills, through forests and past streams for a little more than a mile. You will reach what used to be a logging road for transporting wood from the forest. Go left on this flat, somewhat wide swath, still the Arden-Surebridge Trail. Begin now to look for iron mines. The ones along the trail—which are actually fairly small—look like large holes, averaging maybe 10 feet in diameter, surrounded by rocks and trees. In fact, some hikers might not realize what they are and walk right past them.

Cross a stream and bear left onto a new trail, the Dunning Trail, marked by yellow blazes. This section of the walk is much easier, as you continue along the logging road for a bit. To your left you see the peaceful-looking Pine Swamp, which was a breeding ground for the mosquito plagues the miners had to endure. If you are willing to abandon the trail momentarily in order to locate one of the more spectacular cavelike mines, go up the slope on your right (actually an old tailing pile), until you come to a rocky cliff surrounded by a large mine hole, now filled with water and debris, and a dramatic cave to the left. If you look inside the hillside cave (to which the more intrepid might wish to climb) you will see on your left drill marks from mining days. After exploring this site, return to the yellow flagged trail, which continues on along the swamp. Soon you will come to a fork. If you were to continue on Dunning (yellow) Trail, which is certainly worthwhile but commits you to a much longer hike, you would bear to the right. For our shorter hike we suggest you bear left onto a blue-blaze route, which is part of the Long Path. The trail is somewhat rocky and goes up and down, but is not difficult. You pass through varied scenery of open areas, mountain laurel, forests, streams, and rocky ledges, until you see Lake Skannatati once again, this time on your right. It seems peaceful and inviting, as you wind your way back toward the parking area.

AFTER THE WALK

You might be interested in visiting a restored blast furnace from the heyday of the iron mining era: the Clove Furnace Historic Site, once called Greenwood Furnace, then Arden Furnace. The operation began in 1854, to make iron for Civil War cannons. It thrived until 1885 when it was converted to a dairy farm. This site includes a number of buildings from its various lives. Among them: the impressive furnace itself, two stone silos from the place's farm days, a quaint but run-down farm building that was once a milk bottling factory, and the turbine building that provided power to operate it. You can walk around the structure and wind your way up a little hill to reach the top, from where the iron ore, limestone, and other necessary ingredients were dumped into the ironworks.

The furnace is open Monday through Friday, from 9:00 A.M. to 5:00 P.M.. For further information call the Orange County Historical Society, 914-351-4696.

To reach the Clove Furnace: after you leave the parking lot at Lake Skannatati, retrace your route north on Seven Lakes Drive. At Tiorati Circle take Arden Valley Road west to Route 17. Turn right (north) on 17 for about one mile. The furnace will be on your right.

27

Walking (and Picking Apples) in an Autumn Orchard
Warwick

HOW TO GET THERE:
From the Major Deegan, take the New York State Thruway north, across the Tappan Zee Bridge to exit 16. Take 17 west to exit 127 and head south on Route 13, which is also called Kings Highway. Three miles south of the town of Sugar Loaf, make a right turn at Four Corners Road and follow signs for Applewood Orchard.

On a crisp autumn day one of our favorite walks is through the orderly rows of apple-laden trees in David Hull's Applewood Orchard. These 160 acres of rolling orchard hillside with distant valley views are an inviting spot for strolling at will, picking apples (several kinds), and admiring the Grandma Moses-style scene. A small pond, picnic tables, and the brilliant shiny red apples weighing down the trees give this setting an old-fashioned American look and feel.

This orchard is one of several in the Warwick area, and its atmosphere makes it by far our favorite. The people who work there are friendly and invited us to wander as we wished. There were a minimum of "do" and "don't" signs (unlike a nearby orchard which forbids just about everything you can think of) and we felt entirely comfortable strolling off among the trees. In fact, the whole region around Applewood is a particularly nice one for wandering. The rolling hills, with their luxuriant fall foliage, and the meadows filled with autumn wildflowers in delicate lavenders and shades of gold make the area look like a picture postcard. There are many nature walks in the vicinity, and only three miles from the orchard is Sugar Loaf, a charming craft village (see below).

While autumn is the obvious time to wander through an orchard and to bring home its bounty, we also recommend the blossom time in the spring for pure beauty. The orchard is open spring, summer and fall, seven days a week, from 9:00 A.M. to 5:00 P.M. This is the perfect family walk, not only because children and adults find apple picking fun, but also because the gentle slopes, dozens of grassy lanes between the trees, and fresh clean air make walking very easy. There are tractor and wagon rides too, for those who don't want to stroll. You can phone the orchard at 914-986-1684 for more information.

THE WALK

When you arrive at Applewood, you'll see a small barn where you can pick up empty apple bags, a map of the orchard, as well as farm produce. The map lays out the area of the orchard, including where to find trees of MacIntosh, Cortland, Rome Beauty, Red Delicious, and Golden Delicious apples. You can plot your route according to the kinds of apples you like, or you can head down the driveway to the oldest house in Orange County—the

Staats House—which was built in 1700 and is at one end of the orchard, and start from there. Stopping for a look over the valley below, you can begin your stroll in the Rome Beauty section of the orchard, and proceed along, plucking apples off the trees as you wish. (Apple pickers—long-handled baskets—are for rent if you're serious about reaching the high ones.) You can walk straight through the orchard, or zig and zag as you wish, ending up at the pond that we found nestled below the trees and surrounded with children who had just come from a tractor ride through the orchard. The man in the barn will estimate the weight of your bag of apples and charge you (very reasonably). If you have picked no apples, that's all right, too.

AFTER YOUR WALK

We have already mentioned Sugar Loaf, and it is indeed a special spot to visit. Known as the "Village of Craftsmen," the tiny settlement includes more than a dozen crafts workshops and galleries, and you can watch the making of candles, jewelry, stained glass, and rag dolls. Sculptors, instrument makers, quilters, and other artists were at work when we were there.

Not far away, on Route 17 at exit 129, is the Museum Village of Orange County, a large outdoor museum, with more than 30 buildings housing demonstrations of crafts and early-American life. After your morning at the apple orchard, these two sites will fit right in to your country outing.

28

A Romantic Riverside Walk
Nyack Beach State Park, Nyack

HOW TO GET THERE:

From Manhattan's west side: West Side Highway, George Washington Bridge, Palisades Interstate Parkway, exit 4, north on Route 9W. From exit 4 you will go about nine miles north to get to Nyack Beach State Park. (After about 5.5 miles you come to a blinker light. Bear right, take Broadway and keep going straight, past the village of Nyack. You will run right into the park. Take the road to the right, down the hill, to the parking area.)

From Manhattan's east side: FDR Drive, Harlem River Drive, George Washington Bridge, and then follow the same directions as above.

This is a beautiful, romantic riverside walk in which the Hudson River is so close you can actually put your feet in at any moment. The winding path is a one-way trail along the riverbank, but you will find it interesting and varied even when you retrace your steps. The red sandstone, shale and traprock cliffs of the Palisades at Hook Mountain border the trail on one side, while the gently lapping river flanks the other.

The trail is totally flat, with occasional picnic tables and lookout rocks. You can go 1.7 miles to the end or do any part of it, remembering that you have to walk back.

This is an all-season walk, although it can be cold and blustery in winter. However, many enjoy it particularly then, when large ice floes dot the river and bang up against the shoreline. Even on the hottest summer days the walk is pleasant, breezy, and partly shaded. In late spring you will find a wonderful variety of wildflowers. As might be expected, Sundays are more crowded, although we have never found it unpleasantly so. The rest of the time it is a mostly quiet, solitary walk.

We recommend this outing for anyone, including families with children. But remember that young children must be kept from the temptation of climbing too high up on the rocky outcroppings.

A WALK ALONG THE HUDSON RIVER BANK

PALISADES INTERSTATE PARK

ROCKLAND LAKE

HUDSON

RIVER

LANDING & ROAD TO LAKE

SHORE WALK

HOOK MT.

BEGIN WALK AT SHORE

NYACK BEACH

UPPER NYACK VILLAGE

NORTH BROADWAY WALK

PETERSON'S BOAT YARD

NYACK

TO RTE 9W and RTE 59

MAIN ST

BROADWAY

ANTIQUE SHOPS and VICTORIAN HOUSE TOUR

FRANKLIN ST

THRUWAY

TAPPAN ZEE BRIDGE

NYACK MARINA

N
W — E
S

Elderly walkers will love this cool, breezy trail.

Bring a picnic, as there are no concessions along the way. Any good, comfortable shoes will do, since you will find the path soft and easy on the feet. This is a fine walk for picture taking or sketching, with the ever-changing river at your side. Some people ride bikes on the trail, while others bring their dogs.

Nyack Beach State Park is open daily from 8:00 A.M. until dusk. There is a small parking fee in season.

THE WALK

Leave your car in the parking area by the river and head north on the narrow cinder trail before you.

If you're walking in late spring you'll enjoy the array of wild-flowers and plants that flank the path on both sides: wild gera-niums, roses, daisies, honeysuckle, wild grape, tall grasses that bend with gentle breezes. There are dramatic clusters of rocks along the mountainside forming majestic cliffs that dominate the landscape. These steep cliffs were quarried in the late 19th century to provide rock for growing New York City. Some 32 quarries cut rock from sites along here; it was then barged down the river to the city.

At every bend you will come to great river views. Take your binoculars and observe life on the river. On Sundays sailboat races are often held, and occasionally you'll spot a Hudson River schooner sailing by. Across the water you can see the historic sites of Washington Irving lore: Philipse Manor and Sleepy Hollow Manor and the village of Ossining, with its formidable Sing Sing prison. To the north you might see Croton, if it's a clear day, and the Croton Point Park jutting out onto the river. On the river itself, in addition to the passing boats, you might spot a variety of ducks or geese swimming by lazily.

Occasionally you'll cross a hidden path going up the hill to the left into Hook Mountain State Park, but we suggest you stay on the main trail, which is the most scenic.

After about one mile you will reach an especially attractive lookout point. If you've taken your dog (they are allowed here as long as they are leashed), this is a good place to let it wade into the Hudson! You can stop and rest at one of the picnic tables here and take in the view.

If you continue north you will come to Landing Road, a fairly steep paved road to the left, which will take you into Rockland Lake State Park (see walk 23). This marks the end of our walk, although you may wish to continue.

If you do go on, after about five minutes' walk up the road you will see a smaller paved path to the right, which goes back down to the river, then north, paralleling the river for several more miles to the town of Haverstraw. On your return you will have the Tappan Zee Bridge before you, as a focus for your walk.

AFTER THE WALK

If you're not tired, you might wish to explore further. From the parking area walk back up the paved road and reenter the park going uphill this time, to the wonderful plateau of Hook Mountain. There are playing fields, more picnic tables, and views galore. This is a great spot for children!

If you are still in the mood for more activity, drive to the village of Nyack, now quite an antique center. Most of the antique (and craft) shops are located on South Broadway from Depew Avenue to Main Street, although there are some on Main Street as well. Sundays are fairly busy, when tourists and collectors arrive en masse. Those who prefer ambling at a more leisurely pace would enjoy strolling through during the week; most of the shops are open Tuesdays through Sundays.

In addition, we suggest you at least catch a glimpse of the following:

1. In Upper Nyack, on your way south from the park, stop and look at the Old Stone Church, the oldest in Rockland County, dating from 1813. The church is located on North Broadway near Birchwood.

2. Petersen's Boatyard on Van Houten Street, off North Broadway, has been functioning since 1898. Although there are no boat rentals, it's fun to browse around.

3. Edward Hopper House, 82 North Broadway, is the boyhood home of the artist Edward Hopper. Built in 1858, it is now a small art gallery that shows works by Rockland County artists. The Hopper House provides short walking tour maps of some of the local places Hopper knew and painted.

Nyack has some special events that might interest you:

There are two annual street fairs, in May and September, featuring arts, crafts, and antiques, when many dealers set up shop on the streets in town. Call 914-358-5234 for information.

On Wednesdays, from early June until Thanksgiving, there is an open-air farmer's market in the municipal parking lot in the center of town at Main and Cedar streets. Here you will find fresh-picked produce. It's best to get there early (soon after 8:30 A.M.), as the market is very popular.

NEARBY CONNECTICUT WALKS

29

A New England Village Walk
Litchfield

HOW TO GET THERE:

From the west side of Manhattan: Henry Hudson Parkway (West Side Highway) to Saw Mill River Parkway to Interstate 684 north Route 84 east to exit 17; north on Route 63 to Litchfield.
From the east side of Manhattan: FDR Drive, Major Deegan Expressway to Saw Mill River Parkway. Follow same directions as above.

This is a walk through a rare, unspoiled New England town. Litchfield is a village that has managed to retain its Colonial character for almost 300 years. The visitor arriving here is astonished by the seemingly endless rows of perfect 18th-century white houses, the elegant Congregational Church poised above the town green, the cobblestone courtyards of shops. But Litchfield is not a reconstruction or a self-conscious preservation effort; it has been able to retain its architectural integrity by vigilant citizen effort and through accidents of geography and history. Yet it is a bustling town with lots to see within a relatively concentrated area.

Litchfield has an illustrious history for such a small place: It was home to the nation's first law school and the first seminary for girls; the 18th-century home of Connecticut's chief justice is found here as well as the 1787 parsonage where Harriet Beecher Stowe's father lived. Litchfield was a small but well-to-do Colonial and Federalist settlement, as can be seen from the grandeur of its early homes.

In 1719 Litchfield was incorporated in the Connecticut Assembly, divided into 60 homesteads each of 15 acres. Some of these can still be visited. The colonists prospered, and soon Litchfield became an important stagecoach stop between Boston and New York, and Albany and New Haven. In 1751 it was chosen to be county seat. By the time of the Revolution, Litchfield, strongly on

VILLAGE
of
LITCHFIELD

the patriot side, provided as many as 500 men to the effort. Among
the Revolutionary tales is one describing how an equestrian statue
of George III was toppled in New York City and dragged all the

way to Oliver Wolcott's woodshed on South Street in Litchfield, where it was melted down into bullets by the local ladies. And, we should add, both Lafayette and Washington slept here—many times.

Litchfield citizens became prominent in many fields. Tapping Reeve (not an original landowner) started the nation's first law school in 1774; among its students were Aaron Burr (Reeve's brother-in-law), three Supreme Court justices, 28 senators, and more than 100 Congressmen. Here Sarah Pierce opened her Female Academy, the first school for young ladies' higher education in the country. By the 1850s, when railroads brought people and prosperity, Litchfield was left behind. In 1859 it was still the only four-horse stagecoach stop on the Naugatuck Road. As it escaped industrialization, it became a haven for retired people, summer visitors, and eventually for commuters attracted by the quiet charms of the village and surrounding hills. In 1913 the White Memorial Foundation incorporated to preserve the area including Bantam Lake; some 5,000 acres are devoted to a bird sanctuary, wild gardens, and recreational facilities. And in 1959 Litchfield itself was designated a historic area. Tapping Reeve's law school and the village green, as well as areas of both North and South streets, are registered National Historic Sites.

For your walk you need not bring anything but comfortable shoes and an interest in architecture, craft shops, and Americana. Pick up a walking tour map at the information center on the village green for a detailed guide to each house. A Colonial architecture guide is a good idea if you're interested in such details as eaves, roof lines, and fan windows.

This walk is not difficult or long (covering about one square mile), and there are many places to stop for refreshment or rest. We recommend it for families, including elderly grandparents, and buffs of history and architecture.

Litchfield is nice at any time of the year. Because of its location at the foot of the Berkshires, the fall foliage is particularly glorious. Nearby attractions at Bantam Lake make it a good summer excursion as well, although summer visitors may find it a bit crowded. There are two special annual events that might make you want to visit at a particular time:

The Fall Foliage Rally, held at White Memorial Foundation on a Sunday in early October, is an event children will especially enjoy. Horses and ponies pull carriages and wagons in a series of races. Children are welcome to ask for free rides between competitions. Call 203-354-6507 for information.

The annual tour of selected historic houses occurs on the second Saturday of July (for a small fee). Call the chamber of commerce at 203-482-6586.

THE WALK

A first glimpse will make you want to explore this picture-postcard New England village, the village green, the broad tree-lined avenues, and the charming side streets. The historic district lies right in the center of town along the green, and North and South streets, which are each about .5 mile long. As mentioned before, we suggest stopping by the information center on the village green to pick up a map. You will walk past stately Colonial homes, uniformly white with black shutters, that have been occupied by governors, justices, and senators through the years, as well as the birthplaces of Ethan Allen, Henry Ward Beecher, and Harriet Beecher Stowe.

Your walk should begin with the church at the green. Proceed along the green by the parsonage (1787), past three small shops from the 1780s, and then north along North Street. At the watering trough, cross the street and start back on the other side, passing five homes, the bank, and the jail. At the green are the Methodist Church and the Court House. Along South Street you will find the Tapping Reeve House (1773) and many other interesting sites:

First Congregational Church is a fine example of the double-octagon steeple design. Built in 1829, it was moved in the 1870s; after functioning as a meeting place and movie house, in 1929 it was returned to its proper site on the green. Open daily.

Litchfield Historical Society and Museum in the Noyes Memorial Building exhibits Revolutionary period paintings, including those of Ralph Earl, as well as some furniture and law books, in an uncluttered and inviting setting. Open April through December, Tuesday through Saturday, from 11:00 A.M. to 5:00 P.M. (203-567-5862).

Tapping Reeve House and Law School, South Street, graduated over 1,000 notable students who contributed greatly to American society, such as Horace Mann, Aaron Burr, and John C. Calhoun. Inside the museum, dedicated to Judge Reeve, you can see fine antique furniture that belonged to the Reeve family and sundry historic mementoes. The tiny schoolhouse next door has on display handwritten ledgers of students and original law books. You can visit from May to October, 11:00 A.M. to 5:00 P.M.

Wolcott Memorial Library, South Street, exhibits paintings, sculpture and photography. Although the main library is new, it is attached to a 1799 house built by Oliver Wolcott, Jr., son of one of the signers of the Declaration of Independence. Open year round, Tuesday through Saturday.

Cobble Court, around the corner from the Historical Museum, is a well-appointed group of small shops featuring local handcrafts, clothing, imported yarns, new and old books, and cookware.

Sheldon's Tavern, North Street is another where spot George Washington actually slept.

AFTER YOUR WALK

Within easy driving distance you'll find several unusual places to visit:

Haight Vineyards and Winery, Chestnut Hill Road, Litchfield, is an unusual 15-acre farm winery operated by a small staff using traditional methods. Tours and tastings are offered free of charge, Wednesday through Saturday from 10:30 A.M. to 4:30 P.M.

White Flower Farm, Route 63, in Morris, is a beautiful nursery that attracts visitors from considerable distances because of its unusual assortment of plants. Open from April 1 through November, its gardens and greenhouses are particularly lovely in late spring and summer. (Call 203-567-9415.)

If you still have energy to spare, you might want to drive to nearby Washington, a hilltop community with wonderful views over miles of valleys with rolling hills, or New Preston and Washington Depot, which are also worth a detour.

White Memorial Foundation and Litchfield Nature Center, off Route 202 and west of Litchfield, is a 4,000-acre nature center and wildlife preserve—the largest in the state—that is particularly popular with birders. With its 11 ponds and the Bantam River, the preserve provides just the right type of environment for over 200 species: grackles, starlings, bluebirds, woodpeckers, goldfinches, crows, owls, wading birds (including herons), to name a few. You can watch birds from a special observatory where you cannot be seen by them.

30

A Hillside Walk in a Revolutionary War Encampment Site
Putnam Memorial State Park, Redding

HOW TO GET THERE:

Major Deegan Expressway to the Merritt Parkway to exit 45 (Connecticut Route 58). Follow Route 58 north for 13.8 miles to its intersection with Route 107. The historic park is on your left where you see the statue. You can leave your car along the side of the road near the entrance.

In 1778–79 General Israel Putnam and his troops of the Continental Army braved the Connecticut winter on this wooded, stony hillside. The encampment made use of the natural caves and protection afforded by the giant boulders, a freshwater spring, and the lookouts over the countryside below. The site still contains the remains of chimneys, the foundations of the officers' huts, and several small reconstructed buildings, which give the visitor the feeling of the time and place. And the natural setting is unusually pretty, with a sparkling lake and fine views, not much different from what they must have been when the sentries looked out over the wooded hillsides for marauding Tories.

If you are a history buff this is an especially nice way to enjoy the rock-strewn Connecticut countryside. We relished the fresh crisp air on the hillside and the nice trails, as well as the feeling of walking in the Continental Army's campsite. We recommend this walk for families with children, particularly if they are old enough to enjoy the historical significance and strong enough to scamper over the many rock formations and rather steep hillside.

There are two parts to this park: one, with the campsite features, is not too large and on the hill; the other is quite flat, around the wooded Lake Putnam where any walker can easily find a nice trail.

This is one of the oldest state parks in Connecticut. About

SOLDIERS HUT

PHILIP'S CAVE

FIREBACKS

MUSEUM

MONUMENT

PARK ENT.

RTE 58

PUTNAM MEMORIAL STATE PARK

RTE 107

RTE 59

TO REDDING

TO MERRITT PKWAY & BRIDGEPORT

TO DANBURY and RTE 84

PARK ENT.

LAKE PUTNAM

N
W — E
S

100 years after the original encampment, it became a memorial park and additions have been made at various times since then. Unlike so many "official" historic sites, this one has a very natural look, though there has been some reconstruction. There is a distinctive statue at the entrance, showing General Putnam riding his horse down steps cut into a cliffside. Made by Anna Hyatt Huntington when she was in her nineties, it sets the tone for the park: it is dignified and heroic, but on a small scale, as were so many battles and encampments of the Revolution. Within the park is a small museum, the Revolutionary War Museum, open from May 15 to September 15, from 9:00 A.M. to 5:00 P.M., and weekends until October 15. It has a nice collection of historical material and a map of the parkland. The park itself is open all year for walking, as are the little hut and reconstruction of the soldiers'

living quarters (some 8 to 12 slept in this tiny, windowless building). Of course, you can view the various pits and foundations at any time.

This is a good outing for a picnic. There are no concession booths or commercial establishments, although there are rest rooms. You are, of course, only a mile or two from the towns of Bethel and Redding where you can get refreshments at a number of places. But the lookouts and picnic areas near the lake are ideal for eating al fresco. You might also want to take your binoculars, as there are great views and many birds, including humming-birds in fall migration. Wear good walking shoes or sneakers if you plan to climb over rocks.

THE WALK

First, park near the entrance to the campsite where you see the Huntington statue. Pick up a map and historical material at the small museum near the gate. The first things you see that suggest the encampment are piles of stones along the edge of the road. These are the remains of the fireplaces and chimneys of the wooden huts of the soldiers. They give an uncanny feeling of the past. As you walk along the bottom of the hillside you will come to a dirt path. Here you'll find an entire chimney from one of the soldiers' huts. If you follow the main roadway, you'll spot a large rocky configuration with steps and railing built alongside. Here natural protection from rain, wind, and snow was afforded the troops by hollows in the rocks and shallow caves. One such cave is called Philip's cave; there is a local legend that after the Revolution a soldier named Philip returned to live there. On your right you'll see a reconstructed officers' barrack, a dark windowless shack with a dirt floor. There are several small paths leading into the woods, which will bring you to lookouts or foundations of other buildings. There is a burial monument to the 15 soldiers who died during the encampment, and there is a stone-lined magazine, where gunpowder or munitions were probably stored. Among these sites are stands of larch or tamarack trees, our only deciduous conifer. In the autumn the needles are golden before they fall, giving the hillside a beautiful glow.

When you have completed your tour, you can return to your car and drive up the road a short distance, this time turning to the right. Here is the adjoining part of Putnam Memorial State Park. It surrounds Lake Putnam, a breathtaking lake with lotus and water lilies floating on it. There are picnic facilities in this part of the park and several pretty nature trails. You can find further signs of the encampment here: both fireback remains and a freshwater spring that probably supplied the soldiers with water.

AFTER THE WALK

You are in an unusually pretty area of Connecticut, with pleasant and scenic drives. For something unusual, visit the Bethel Firefighters Museum, at 36–40 South Street in Bethel.

31

A Walk Through
"The Jewel of Long Island Sound"
Southport

HOW TO GET THERE:

From the west side of Manhattan: West Side Highway, to Cross Bronx Expressway, to Route 95, to exit 19. Follow signs to Southport.
From the east side of Manhattan: FDR Drive to the Major Deegan which becomes Route 95, and follow same directions as above.

This elegant little village, with its scenic harbor on the Sound, is about an hour away from New York City. It is ideal for walking, with its pleasant winding roads and salt smell of the sea. You're never more than several blocks from the water. Impeccable 19th-century homes and fine old trees line the streets; its historic district was the first designated in Connecticut. Unlike more bustling waterfront communities such as nearby Fairfield, Southport seems to sit firmly in the 19th century. It has been able to resist commercial expansion and to retain an unusually peaceful flavor.

The Indians sold their claims to Southport in 1661 for "13 coats, two yards apiece, and ye rest in wampum." "Mill River," as it was then called, was at first a prosperous farming area. It began to develop into a village around the time its shipyard was built in 1763. Its natural harbor was small but deep enough to handle ships of up to 100 tons, and it provided surrounding towns with imported luxuries. The local population included wealthy merchants, sea captains, and shipowners. The William Bulkley House at 824 Harbor Road, probably the oldest on the harbor, dates from this period (c. 1760). However, Mill River's prosperity was temporarily disrupted during the Revolutionary War when the British burned much of the port, leaving only a single building.

In the early decades of the 19th century, Mill River became a more commercial port, home to five schooners, 20 sloops, and one brig. There are still some buildings left from this period. Along Harbor Road you can see several old warehouses that have been converted to residences. In addition, you should note the Gurdon Perry House (c. 1830) at 780 Harbor Road and the Austin Perry House (c. 1830) at 712 Harbor Road.

Soon the town and harbor were growing rapidly and becoming so prosperous that some of the residents even had their own fleets of vessels that sailed to faroff places in the Orient, Europe, or South America. Onion farming was developed in the 19th century and eventually became the town's main source of wealth, bringing the village the nickname "onion capital of America." Southport onions even helped prevent scurvy among the troops during the Civil War.

In the late 19th century the town began to attract New Yorkers looking for a pleasant place to spend the summer. Several fine mansions, as well as the Romanesque-style Pequot Library, date from the Victorian period. Southport became an affluent residential suburb, as new estates were built in the Green Farms and Sasco Hill areas. The Pequot Yacht Club became (and remains) the center of the harbor front.

If you enjoy strolling through lanes of graceful old houses with widow's walks amid gentle seaside breezes, you'll like this walk. A history of Southport called "Walking Through History" is available at the Fairfield Historic Society in Fairfield.

Southport is a noncommercial town, not geared for tourists. You are welcome to walk through, but you won't find any restaurants, public bathing, or other tourist facilities. Take a picnic, or go to Sherman Green's Firehouse Deli on Reef Road (off the Post Road just before the center of Fairfield) for picnic makings. Practically next door is Allington's Ice Cream Manufactury, which we recommend for dessert. Visit the farm stand on Post Road for fresh fruit, and then drive to Jennings Beach in Fairfield for a picnic right on the Sound. You might also take a bathing suit, if you decide to drive to Fairfield's Jennings Beach later.

This is an American village walk with its own distinctive flavor. You can easily do this outing in an hour or so, and anyone seeking a real Yankee seaside village walk will enjoy Southport. It's easy on the feet and the energy and relatively simple to reach. Since the boating and swimming facilities are not available to visitors (unless, of course, you arrive by boat), it may be frustrating to small children—even if you promise to go swimming or sailing later.

We recommend that you visit in summer, although spring and fall are lovely too. Special events that might persuade you to go at a particular time include:

Dogwood Festival. This one-week spring festival takes place in the nearby town of Greenfield Hill (Old Academy and Bronson Roads). The festival is a week-long celebration featuring the 30,000 dogwoods, some of which were originally transplanted after the Revolution. The festival takes place under a tent on the green, features concerts, art shows, sales, and walking tours. Call 203-259-2128 for the exact date and/or luncheon reservations.

Fairfield Day. Celebrated at Jennings Beach on the last Sunday in June, when the town of Fairfield sponsors children's races, egg throwing, musical entertainment, clowns, and even a sky-diving exhibition. No admission charge. Arrive before 11:00 A.M. to avoid traffic and parking problems. Call 203-367-8495 for further information.

THE WALK

In addition to the houses listed below, you should visit the harbor, the focal point of the village. Put your feet in the water! Just viewing Long Island Sound from the coast of Connecticut is a pleasure on a nice day. Southport and some of its surrounding villages have nice waterfronts for watching tides change, boats coming and going, or gulls soaring overhead. Look for seaweed, barnacles, mussels, clams, and other marine life along the sandy coast of the Sound. Gulls and water fowl abound.

For the walk through town, start at the corner of Westway and Harbor roads. (Numbers are keyed to map.)

1. William Bulkley House (c. 1760) at 824 Harbor Road is one of the oldest houses still standing on Southport harbor. It is called a "three-quarters house" meaning that there are four bay windows in the front instead of the more usual five. The house has recently been restored.

2. Old storehouses (early 19th century) at 789 and 825 Harbor Road have been converted to residences. Number 789 was also used as a clubhouse for the Pequot Yacht Club.

3. Gurdon Perry House (c. 1830) at 780 Harbor Road belonged to a wealthy merchant in the early part of the 19th century. An unpretentious house, it is simpler in style than many later homes built for merchants.

4. Austin Perry House (c. 1830) at 712 Harbor Road is particularly interesting for its portico, which is considered one of the finest of its kind, probably dating from the 1840s.

5. Pequot Yacht Club (c. 1835) at 669 Harbor Road was a warehouse during the port's commercial peak.

6. Jennings Store Building (c. 1834 and later) at 668–70 Harbor Road included the town's first general store and post office. Sections were added during the Victorian period, when the second

floor was used as a reading room before the Pequot Library was built.

7. Southport National Bank (1833) at 227 Main Street is now a private residence. Note its Greek Revival style.

8. Hall block and chronicle buildings (1894) at 244 and 252 Main Street were once tenements that housed stores and offices. They were converted into apartments in the 1950s.

9. Southport Savings Bank (1865) at 226 Main Street was built to resemble the roof pitch of the Episcopal Church.

10. Oliver Bulkley House (1859) at 176 Main Street is a wonderful example of early Gothic architecture. For some years this house was called the Pequot Inn; it was used by summer boarders in the 1920s until it was converted into a private home. Note its lovely grounds.

11. Charles M. Gilman House (1873) at 139 Main Street is an interesting combination of Italianate and Gothic styles.

12. Old Academy (1827) at 95 Main Street has served in many capacities. First a private school, it then held church services and finally became a private home in the late 19th century.

13. Pequot Library (c. 1894), located at the intersection of Westway and Pequot Avenue, was designed by a student of H. H. Richardson in Romanesque style and donated to the village.

14. Trinity Episcopal Church (1862), on the corner of Pequot Avenue and Center Street, was built in the Carpenter Gothic style after its original structure (virtually identical) was destroyed by a tornado. The church has a lovely slender spire that can be seen for miles.

AFTER YOUR WALK

There are many odd and amusing places in the vicinity of Southport. Jennings Beach (off Fairfield Beach Road in Fairfield), a wide expanse of nice sandy beach with pleasantly choppy seas, is well worth a visit.

The Birdcraft Museum, 314 Uniquowa Road, Fairfield, has a collection of 2,000 mounted birds and mammal specimens on display, as well as some 50 decoys.

The Old Burying Ground in Fairfield has many pre-Revolutionary gravestones, some carved with angels, skulls, or willows. Bring your own grave rubbing materials, or pick some up at the several art supply stores in Fairfield. The cemetery is located along Beach Road.

Sherwood Island is a state-owned facility off Westport with large bathhouses, just west of Southport (the quickest route is back onto the Connecticut Turnpike to Sherwood Island exit and across the causeway to the beach). It is somewhat crowded in season.

P.T. Barnum Museum, 820 Main Street, Bridgeport, dedicated to the great circus showman is fun, from the curiosities inside—such as a 50,000-piece model circus and Tom Thumb memorabilia—to the architecture itself, with its dome-shaped and "eyebrow" dormers. If you're a circus fan, this flamboyant museum is a good stop. To get there, take I-95 to exit 27, turn toward downtown Bridgeport and Main Street.

United House Wreckers is another amusing stop. Many people are addicted to junk, but even if you just like antiques and old things from bygone eras you should not miss United House Wreckers in Stamford on your way home. U.H.W. is at 535 Hope Street in Stamford (203-348-5371). It consists of acres, literally, of salvaged items, from marble mantelpieces to old bathtubs, from the smallest antique rings to giant bulls that once stood outside beef restaurants. You can find furniture, sculpture, ancient instruments, chandeliers from a famous lobby—you name it! Whatever someone else might have disposed of, United House Wreckers has chosen to save. Some of it is indoors, some outdoors.

NEARBY
PENNSYLVANIA
WALKS

A Medicinal Trail Walk
*Bowman's Hill State Wildflower Preserve,
Washington's Crossing*

HOW TO GET THERE:

*New Jersey Turnpike to exit 9. Take Route 1 south toward Trenton.
Pick up Route 95 (295) south after Princeton (at Bakersville) and
take the highway to the exit at Yardley, Pa. Turn back to Route
32 and travel a few miles until you reach Bowman's Hill Preserve.*

This unusual walk is along a trail devoted to plants that have
real—or legendary—uses as medicines. A part of the lovely Bowman's Hill Wildflower Preserve, the medicinal trail is a special
walk for herb fanciers and those who are interested in natural
curing or Indian herb uses. In our country the Indians often used
herbal medicines, and modern science has frequently verified
their effectiveness. Some have even been synthetically repro-
duced. Many plants are still used in pharmacology, but others are
of no proven value—their curative properties are nothing more
than old-wives' tales. The medicinal trail includes some of each
kind, with a descriptive flier that tells you what you're seeing and
what it's good for—or what legends say it's good for.

The trail, which is about 620 feet long, is slow going, if you
stop to examine each plant. While you are warned not to taste
anything yourself—some of the plants are extremely poisonous—
you are encouraged to go slowly and study each plant's story as
you go.

The trail begins with mountain laurel, the juices of which the
Indians supposedly drank to commit suicide (but by 1800 a tinc-
ture made from its leaves was being used to treat several diseases).
Next comes mayapple and bloodroot, a source of morphine that
Indians chewed to cure a sore throat. Other plants include white
oak, spicebush, wild ginger, alumroot, fairywand, and witch hazel.
Among the old wives' varieties is ginseng, which Europeans

thought restored youth (and which has been used for centuries as a cure-all in China). The list is a fairly long one, and a walk along these plants is extremely interesting.

This outing, due to the dangerous nature of many of the plants, is not recommended for small children, particularly if you read the more disturbing legends aloud.

For other walks in Bowman's Hill Wildflower Preserve, see walk 33, which can of course be combined with this walk on the same day. There are a tree identification trail, wildflower trails and several kinds of nature walks in this preserve. Several times during the year the preserve offers guided mushroom walks, bird walks, native plant and fern identification walks, as well as other wild plant walks.

The preserve is open year round, except for major holidays. Each season brings different plantings and appropriate events.

For "After Your Walk" see the suggestions following walk 33.

33

A Walk in a Wildflower Preserve
Bowman's Hill State Wildflower Preserve, Washington's Crossing

HOW TO GET THERE:

New Jersey Turnpike to exit 9. Take Route 1 south toward Trenton. Pick up Route 95 (295) south after Princeton (at Bakersville) and take the highway to the exit at Yardley, Pa. Turn back to Route 32. Bowman's Hill Preserve is several miles northwest on Route 32.

As you walk along the woodsy trails and gentle creek in this lovely spot you'll feel you are miles from the bustle of the highway and civilization. The preserve has managed to include in its 100 acres quite a variety of habitats—forest, meadows, ponds, bogs, an arboretum, and preserves for shrubs and flowers. An azalea trail leads to a path of bluebells, a marsh walk brings you to marigolds and holly areas, you pass the charming dam on the Pidcock Creek and come to the evergreen area. The list is extensive, and the walk—quite hilly—is always interesting. You can choose your own paths—up and down and around about—with the help of a map and a variety of printed guides that are available near the parking area. We found it quite uninhabited in midsummer, but spring with its profusion of wildflowers is apt to be a bit busier. However, there is enough room for many walkers, and the trails are woodsy enough to absorb a fair number of people. The more energetic can hike to the famous Bowman's Hill Tower at the top of a surprisingly high hill in the preserve (or drive there), and complete their visit to this historic and lovely place.

Established to preserve Pennsylvania's native plants, Bowman's Hill opened in 1934. It is made up of 26 trails, including a trail for the handicapped (wheelchair accessible) and a famous arboretum called Penn's Woods, which has more than 450 different trees and shrubs. The general atmosphere of Bowman's Hill Preserve is relaxed. It is rather like wandering through a large private

19th-century estate. There are few signs telling you what to do or not to do, and the fences and steps are made of natural materials that seem to have fallen in place by accident. The signs identifying the various walks and plants are almost hidden by foliage and are never obtrusive, so you don't feel as if you are in a preserve but in a series of natural habitats.

Pick up a guide to the various walks and a tree and flower guide to the preserve at the headquarters where you leave your car. You might want to take your own identifying books, too. Insect repellent, stout shoes, and a picnic are all recommended.

This walk, particularly if you climb to the lookout tower, can be rigorous. But if you want more gentle trails, the preserve has those as well. We recommend this outing for anyone who enjoys wildflowers, woods, and hiking. It is ideal for children, who can roam freely.

The preserve is open year round except for major holidays. Of course wildflowers are best in spring and early summer, but there is something to be seen in any season.

THE WALK

When you drive to Bowman's Hill Preserve, you will pass a picnic ground and public facilities near the entrance. Keep going and leave your car at the lot behind the headquarters. You can choose which of 26 trails you wish to take, but most run into one another and you can't go wrong whichever you take. If you go down hill from the car park, you will come to the creek, which you can follow along its winding path. If you continue along the roadway (not accessible to cars) to its end, you will come to a rugged climb to Bowman's Tower. If you go back in the direction of the entrance you can walk through the arboretum. All of the trails should be seen, and the total walk is not beyond most walkers' endurance.

Among the nine acres of woods are familiar sugar maples, pitch pines, and American lindens, as well as the more rare chinquapin chestnut, cucumber magnolia, paw paw, and black haw. There are also a medicinal plant trail (see walk 32) and an educational nature trail.

Bowman's Hill Tower stands on a hill 380 feet above sea level—one of the highest points along the Delaware River. The hill has long served as a landmark, and before Washington's crossing of the Delaware it was used as a lookout and signal station. The present tower commands a view of 14 miles of the Delaware River Valley, including the very spot that Washington crossed. The tower can be visited and climbed (every day but Tuesday) year round. There is a small admission fee.

The hike up to the tower takes you through some rather dense underbrush, but your effort is well rewarded at the top. If you prefer, you can get back in your car and drive out of the preserve, go back onto Route 32, turning to the right as you exit, and you will soon come to a sign to the tower. A winding drive brings you to a parking area at its base. The spectacular view from the tower is a fitting end to your walk.

AFTER THE WALK

Washington's Crossing State Park. Directly across Route 32 from Bowman's Hill Preserve is the historic site where General Washington crossed the Delaware on Christmas 1776. You can see the banks the Continental Army climbed, the houses where they rested, and you can take a tour and watch a short documentary film at Memorial Auditorium. The state park is on both sides of the Delaware River and includes all sorts of park facilities, from cooking areas to picnic grounds, to a Braille nature trail. This is an especially tasteful historic site, and walking through it gives a real sense of time and place. It has not been "hoked up" and we like its simplicity. Most buildings are open year round, 9:00 A.M. to 4:30 P.M. There are small fees for park use, but not for the historic sites.

Among the places we recommend you visit in the park are:

Thompson-Neeley House, known as the House of Decision, where Washington's strategy is said to have been decided.

The Point of Embarkation. Nice paths will allow you to walk to the exact spot of the crossing.

The Old Ferry Inn. Open year-round, this 1757 inn is thought to have fed the general before he set off across the river; it is still furnished in the style of that time.

Lambertville, N.J. Lambertville is New Hope's across-the-river neighbor, about six miles northwest on Route 32 and across the bridge. While New Hope has become a very touristy town, Lambertville prides itself on retaining a historic charm. And it is indeed a delightful place to walk and poke into with its small old-fashioned streets and riverside spots. While wandering around, you should not miss the James Wilson Marshall House at 60 Bridge Street. A Registered National Historic Landmark, it was the boyhood home of the man who discovered gold in California in 1848, which led to the famous Gold Rush. Built in 1816 in the Federal style, it is now a museum that displays pictures, maps, and artifacts showing 19th-century life in Lambertville, etc. Open 1:00 to 5:00 P.M. Thursday and Saturday, April 1 through November 15. (Call 609-397-0770 for further information.)

If you prefer a more bustling environment, New Hope across the bridge from Lambertville is a mecca of shops and entertainment. For a listing of things to do and see in New Hope, see walk 34.

If you still feel energetic after your day at Bowman's Hill Preserve and want more active recreation, the Delaware River is the perfect place to be. Water sports are easily available in the area you are in. Among the possibilities:

Canoeing on the Delaware is world famous. What makes it so attractive is that the Delaware is one of the last free-flowing rivers and is portage free for 185 miles, from Hancock, N.Y., to Trenton, N.J. In addition, it is one of the last of the wild and scenic rivers in the East and has a great abundance of wildlife. One of the most efficiently organized places nearby where you can rent canoes or plan excursions is Point Pleasant Canoe Outfitters at Point Pleasant, Pa. (a few miles north of New Hope on Route 32). Call 215-297-8400/8181 for further information.

Fishing and inner tubing are also popular in the Delaware River.

34

A Towpath Walk Along the Delaware Canal
From New Hope

HOW TO GET THERE:

New Jersey Turnpike to exit 9. Take Route 1 south toward Trenton. Pick up Route 95 (295) south after Princeton (at Bakersville) and take the highway to the exit at Yardley, Pa. Take Route 32 West to New Hope.

The level towpath that runs alongside this picturesque canal is an ideal walking route. Originally built to accommodate the mules that pulled barges along the canal—as they still do today—the towpath is narrow and overhung with trees; it is a scenic delight as it winds along the waterway. It is flat for walking, and the only impediments to a solitary walk are occasional joggers and bikers and other walkers, in addition to the mules who still ply the canal drawing barges now filled with sight-seers.

If you start at its beginning, the canal walk can cover almost 60 miles, and as a matter of fact, hardy walkers do just that, either taking their camping gear along, or sleeping at inns along the route. Our chosen walk is quite a bit shorter, though you can lengthen it at will, particularly if you have a car parked at the other end. It is especially nice on a spring day, when the willow trees along the way are at their lightest green, and when the canal seems bright and clean.

Keep in mind as you walk that you are never very far from civilization, and you can turn off the towpath now and again for refreshment at a nearby village. We preferred, however, to stay on the path, taking a picnic lunch with us.

As we mentioned above, spring is the ideal time for this walk, although fall is also very pleasant. Summer finds New Hope such a tourist mecca that we hesitate to add more people to the crush. The towpath is always open, so even winter walkers can use it if they enjoy the crisp waterside winds.

There are no restrictions on visitors to the towpath, or on what they take along. You can bring your dog, a picnic, and whatever else you would like to have. We suggest strong walking shoes and birding binoculars.

This canal, which is steeped in history, covers an area of Pennsylvania that is beautiful both in natural scenery and in architecture. The old stone houses for which Pennsylvania is well known sit smack along the towpath, surrounded by giant sycamores, tulip poplars, locusts, oaks, and overhanging weeping willows. Rhododendrons and hill laurel abound—another reason to go in spring. Fishermen enjoy the canal for catfish, perch, and carp, in addition to small-mouthed black bass that have traditionally been caught here. Shad, once a flourishing crop, are just beginning to make a comeback.

Birders will be well rewarded on this walk. Among the waterfowl seen at any time of year are mallard and black ducks and night herons; summertime brings egrets and ospreys. Other birds to look for are owls, downy woodpeckers, Carolina wrens, ruffed grouse, marsh hawks, ring-necked pheasants, and turkey vultures, in addition to the more common robins, cardinals, and goldfinches. In summer you might see—or at least hear—whippoorwills. The profusion of birds along the canal is due to its proximity to the Delaware River, which serves as a guide to migratory birds—in particular to Canada geese; they can sometimes be heard honking in early mornings as they wing their way along.

THE WALK

Begin this section of the canal walk at New Hope, a jumble of antique shops, historic houses, and tourist spots in a scenic location along the Delaware River. The canal goes right through New Hope and the towpath is easily reached just east of Merchant Street. (You might want to see lock no. 8 in New Hope before setting out.) Walk out of town along the path heading west. You will first pass the New Hope and Ivyland Railroad, which runs a steam train excursion on weekends in the tourist season. As you leave the bustle of New Hope, you will come to Rabbit Run Bridge, and then in about 1.5 miles to Phillips Mill, built as a grist mill in 1756. Once a thriving art colony, Phillips Mill is now a small community surrounding the converted mill—a nice place to take a breather. About .5 mile farther you can spot the remains of two old kilns where the lime industry once flourished; here lime was mixed to make mortar and crop fertilizer. About three miles from New Hope you'll come to Center Bridge, once known as Readings Ferry (named for Colonel John Reading who established the first Delaware River ferry in 1711). At that time a major route from New York to Philadelphia crossed here. When you reach Center Bridge, cross over to see Stockton in New Jersey, known for its fine stone houses. There is an inn on each side of the water here. (About a mile farther on the New Jersey side you'll find route 519, which leads to a fine covered bridge.)

The sight-seeing barge stops at a picnic area surrounded by rhododendron, where there are picnic tables, grills, and a comfort station. In the center of the canal is Hendricks Island, which virtually fills up the canal. You will now have walked just under five miles. If you continue (assuming you have a car waiting for you), you can walk on to Lumberville, where there is another lock and nice scenery (about two miles along from your picnic site). From there go to Point Pleasant (two more miles), where you'll find the remains of a river bridge and a sandy swimming beach on the Delaware. The walk continues for many miles, eventually ending at Easton, Pa., where the Lehigh River meets the Delaware.

If you prefer to begin the canal walk before New Hope, try combining a visit to Washington's Crossing and Bowman's Hill Preserve (see walk 32) and walking west to join up with this walk at New Hope.

AFTER YOUR WALK

After (or before) explore New Hope and its across-the-river neighbor, Lambertville. The ferry between the two villages was built in 1726 and was known as Coryell's Ferry. You can still visit the site; other historic reminders of the importance of this area in the Revolutionary War are all around, from Washington's Crossing about three miles east, to several historic houses in New Hope.

The boats used by General Washington in the crossing of the Delaware were hidden on a small island in the Delaware near Lambertville, and the hill called Goat Mountain, just to the south of the village, was where Washington was taken to view the island and make sure the boats could not be seen. The Parry Barn Museum in New Hope (Main Street) is a fine 18th-century mansion built at the end of the Revolution and now operated by the New Hope Historical Society.

Reminders of the busy days of canal traffic also still exist: in New Hope you can take the canal-barge ride mentioned above. For information, contact the New Hope Barge Company at 215-862-2842 for a one-hour excursion—a charming and leisurely outing, accompanied on occasion by a folksinger or tale-teller. You can also take a river sight-seeing trip in a small boat from Coryell's ferry landing in Lambertville. For a train ride on one of the few remaining coal-burning trains around, try the excursion line mentioned above; it goes puffing along for 14 miles through scenic Bucks County, beginning in New Hope.

Those interested in historic houses and architecture might enjoy one of the various walking tours of New Hope with its many shops (pick up the guide at the Parry Barn Museum or any shop, or just walk along Ferry, Main, and Bridge streets).

Also worth a visit is the well-known Bucks County Playhouse, which presents professional summer stock in a 250-year-old gristmill on the water. For information call 215-862-2041. A play can be a nice way to end a day of canal walking and exploring a bustling village.

If, however, you are still feeling energetic, you might want to try one of the many water sports that the Delaware River Valley offers. There is canoeing (this is one of the prime canoe spots on the East Coast, and access to the canal can be gained in practically every village), inner tubing, white-water rafting, and fishing. For more information on these sports, call 215-297-8400/8181, Point Pleasant Canoe Outfitters, who can advise you when, where, and how to go about it.

BIRD WATCHING WALKS

35

Birding, Beaching, and Hiking
Off-Season on Sandy Hook
Sandy Hook, N.J.

HOW TO GET THERE:

George Washington Bridge to Route 80 to Garden State Parkway south. Get off at exit 117 to New Jersey 36, to Atlantic Highlands. Go across the bridge to Sandy Hook.
From midtown take Lincoln Tunnel to the New Jersey Turnpike to Garden State Parkway and follow same directions as above.

Sandy Hook, part of the Gateway National Recreation Area, is a narrow spit of land more than seven miles long. Its sandy beach faces the Atlantic on one side; its marshes and bay side face the mainland of the Jersey shore. Although it was developed by the New Jersey state park system as a public beach (on the ocean side), it has been left as an ecosystem of fragile marshland and tidal pools on the bayside. In between is a long roadway with occasional parking areas and ranger station. If you visit Sandy Hook at a non-swimming time, you'll be amazed by the size of the area that has been left in its natural state. Off-season or on a rainy day you're not apt to meet many people hiking on either length of the Hook.

The ocean side of Sandy Hook has a wide beach with nice rolling breakers and the usual miscellaneous Atlantic flotsam, particularly out of season. A walk beginning at the first parking lot, either along the sand (hard walking except close by the waterline), and/or on the top section of the flat rock breakwater at beach's edge, can take you seven miles.

If you are a birder you will prefer the other side of this narrow spit of land, for once you make your way to the bay side, you'll be on a small shell-covered beach, which winds in and out of the bay inlets, depending on the tides. Birds are everywhere. Hundreds of gulls and other sea birds live along this coast, making

167

raucous noise and generally enjoying the carefully preserved eco-system. The marshlands are mostly closed to the public, but if you take your binoculars you can see all kinds of birds swooping in and out of the dune grass and waterfront.

Sand spits like Sandy Hook are buffeted by winds and waves. The vegetation that grows on barrier beaches like this is diverse; beach plum, prickly pear cactus, dusty miller—and large amounts of poison ivy—are indigenous. Also growing here is a holly forest (that can only be seen on special tours given by the park system), an oddity that is part of the closed environment. Some of the holly trees are thought to be more than 300 years old, and their red berries keep many birds wintering here. Both prickly pear and beach heather also proliferate, despite the harsh sandy soil.

Out of season you'll find Sandy Hook an especially fine place to enjoy the Atlantic coastline. In clear weather you can see the buildings of New York City, and yet you're in such a wonderful, natural spot!

This walk is as unhilly as a sandflat and is ideal for any walker. Kids will enjoy beachcombing the waterfront (on both sides), and the great windy openness of the area. Take your own food and drink, your binoculars, a good windbreaker, and shoes that can get sandy or wet.

The park is open year-round. Summer is not recommended for walkers or birders—except on rainy days—because beach traffic is so heavy at this most northern of New Jersey's shorefronts. During the season there is a parking fee; off-season there is no charge and absolutely no congestion. The only visitors you are likely to encounter are fishermen. Sandy Hook is good birding and hiking whenever you go: in fall you'll see waterfowl and shorebirds heading south, the marsh shrubs turning color, and great sunsets. In winter you'll enjoy beachcombing on the ocean side, and spotting ducks, herring, and black-back gulls, as well as occasional kittiwake or gannet. Spring walkers, particularly early in the morning, will see shore birds in breeding plumage, war-blers, hawks, kestrels, even peregrine falcons in migrating season. Songbird and raptor flights are common in April and May.

Remember that an ocean wind is a cold wind, so bundle up if you come in winter or early spring.

U.S. COAST GUARD STATION

FORT HANCOCK

BEACH

NORTH

SANDY HOOK

SHOREBIRD NESTING AREA

BEACH WALK

HORSESHOE COVE

ROADWAY

RANGER STATION

OCEAN

TOWNS of HIGHLANDS and ATLANTIC HIGHLANDS

RARITAN BAY

SKELETON HILL

SPERMACETI COVE

BAY WALK

VISITOR CENTER

BEACHES

ATLANTIC OCEAN

TWIN LIGHTS

THE WALK

There are several ways to walk Sandy Hook. We suggest you begin by driving to the information station first, to pick up a map of the various sections. The beach and bay walk (best for birders) is around Spermaceti Cove (named for a beached whale long ago). To take this walk, park at Lot C, cross the road, and go down to the bay side. Birds you should look for here include some 267 species, of which 49 are considered unusual. Rare or endangered birds include the grebe, gannet, Wilson's phalarope, Hudsonian godwit, osprey (which nests on Sandy Hook), black rail, roseate tern, white-rumped sandpiper, among others. Breeding birds include the clapper rail, the great horned owl, whippoorwill, common flicker, barn swallow, robin, towhee, fish crow, and the brown thrasher. Gulls and other common waterbirds are everywhere.

Other seasonal wildlife to look for: horseshoe crabs in warm weather, which arrive on the beach to spawn; monarch butterflies, which come in droves to feed on the fall goldenrod on their way to wintering in Mexico; brant (small geese), which winter close to the bay shoreline; and some 50,000 broadbills (scaup), which drift and feed in rafts.

There is a shorebird nesting colony on the ocean side some two miles north of the Spermaceti Cove. Those walking along the ocean will be able to spot more birds there. The Old Dune Trail, which begins near the visitors' center, will also take you through a bird viewing area. Guided tours of ecological interest are also available. Inquire at the visitors' center, or call 201-872-0115.

If you prefer ocean beach walking to birding, try parking your car at Area D and setting off away from civilization. You'll find even fewer people and less trammeled beach. Look along the beach for flotsam, or simply enjoy the incoming waves and changing color of the ocean. Of course, if you can arrange to have a car waiting for you at the far end of your walk, you can go on for miles and miles.

AFTER THE WALK

At the farther end of Sandy Hook is Fort Hancock, which has both a lighthouse and museum. But we found the most interesting nearby attraction to be Twin Lights. If you look back toward shore from the beginning of Sandy Hook you'll see two rather ancient looking lighthouses high on the hill. Twin Lights was constructed in 1828 as the Navesink Light Station. The towers, which are not identical, are some 256 feet above sea level. If your legs are still agile after your walk, you can climb the towers (about 65 steps) and get a great view. If you don't want to climb, you can still enjoy a nice display at Twin Lights, which we recommend. Here, one of the first wireless transmissions in America went out, when Marconi telegraphed reports in 1899 of the America's Cup race off Sandy Hook. There are also exhibits about lighthouse lenses, shore boats, and other nautical subjects concerning this once very dangerous coastal area. To get to Twin Lights, retrace your route to the town of Atlantic Highlands and make your way up the winding roads to the top of the hill.

36

Birding in a New Jersey Highland
Scherman-Hoffman Wildlife Sanctuary, Bernardsville, N.J.

HOW TO GET THERE:

From the George Washington bridge take Route 80 to Route 287 south. Exit from 287 at Bernardsville, go west, past intersection with Route 202 and proceed on Child's Road to Hardscrabble Road (turn right). Continue up the hill to the Hoffman Center— or go left a short distance to the Scherman Center. These twin centers' trails intersect, but you can start from either place.

These 240 acres of rolling countryside, dogwood trees, and waving grass are a particularly nice birding spot. Administered by the Audubon Society with a minimum of signs or intrusions, the sanctuary provides a series of hillside trails through wood and field and along streams that are a delight to birder and stroller alike.

The Hoffman section at the top of the hill provides a typically highland environment for native birds, while the adjoining Scherman section includes the lower-lying riverside habitat, so a visit here can give you a chance to spot a great variety of birds.

In fact, more than 125 species have been sighted at this location. Both land birds and water birds are familiar in the sanctuary. In addition, the centers offer a variety of programs dealing with birding, as well as guided field trips in rainy or sunny weather. For those with other naturalistic interests, the centers feature tree and lichen identification workshops and a variety of other programs.

This site is one of nine sanctuaries and five nature centers that the New Jersey Audubon Society administers. In each of these, a different variety of habitat means different sorts of birding, as well as diverse kinds of strolling. This walk is somewhat hilly for elderly walkers, but very nice for families with energetic kids.

The rough state of the walkways through the woods and the rolling terrain make this a slightly strenuous walk, but you can go slowly, of course. Wear boots or wet-shoes (particularly in spring), and take binoculars and your lunch for a wonderful day's outing. The centers are open from 9:00 A.M. to 5:00 P.M. Tuesday through Saturday, and noon to 5:00 P.M. on Sunday.

THE WALK

Leave your car at either of the two centers, depending on whether you prefer the riverside or the more hilly woods. A trail map is available at both spots. Among the birds to look for are migrating land birds in the spring, including robins, and bluebirds and many types of warbler; in fall you'll spot darkeyed juncos, tufted titmice, chickadees, white-throated sparrows, cardinals, and (circling overhead) turkey vultures and red-tailed hawks. Down at the water's edge you might find wood ducks, great blue herons, and kingfishers. This is an excellent spot to visit in springtime when the dogwoods are in bloom and the migrant birds are arriving. As we go to press, a screech owl is making this area his home.

For a list of events, programs, and daily sightings call 201-766-5787.

Other sites in New Jersey offer a different variety of birds. See walk 37 for birding in the Great Swamp and walk 35 for spotting the shore birds at Sandy Hook. In addition, we recommend two: The Lorimer Sanctuary at 790 Ewing Avenue in Franklin Lakes attracts lakeside birds in northern Bergen County (about 35 minutes from the city). Call 201-891-2185 for information. Owl Haven Nature Center, which specializes in these nocturnal creatures, is located at Tennent, N.J., between Englishtown and Freehold. You can visit in the afternoon and see the resident owls (indoors) or walk through the fields and woods of the center to spot an occasional owl and other birds indigenous to the area. Phone 201-780-7007 to find out what birds are in the region and when the center is best for a visit.

37

Bird Watching in the Great Swamp
Morris County, N.J.

HOW TO GET THERE:
George Washington Bridge to Route 80 west to Route 287 south. Get off at exit 26A and follow signs for The Great Swamp National Wildlife Refuge.

The Great Swamp National Wildlife Refuge—a vast (over 6,000 acres) area of swamp woodland, hardwood ridges, marsh, grassland, brush, ponds, and pasture land only 26 miles west of New York City—is a rare environment in which to view birds and other wildlife. This rich land was destined to become the site of an airport in the late 1950s. Fortunately, a band of local citizens and others joined forces, raised funds, and donated the bulk of the swamp property to the U.S. Department of the Interior to guarantee that it would remain forever wild.

Since the late 1960s the swamp has been designated as a wilderness area, a refuge for more than 200 species of birds, as well as for a surprisingly large variety of mammals, reptiles, and amphibians. The fact that it is a "wilderness area" means that motorized traffic is forbidden in certain sections and severely restricted in others, making parking limited and access somewhat difficult. It also means that only the more determined birders and nature watchers roam through the fairly remote trails in this vast terrain, experiencing a true wilderness habitat with its rich variety of migratory birds and other animals. But you can also drive through the refuge or walk on marked trails.

There are two different ways to go birding in the Great Swamp. Within the swamp there is a Wildlife Observation Center off Long Hill Road. Here you can observe and photograph birds and other animals from blinds set in the surrounding boardwalk trails. Organized tours are occasionally conducted for those who prefer going in a group. This center is within a wildlife management area, where research studies are conducted, grasslands and brush are occasionally cut back to ensure the best habitat for the diversity of species, and nesting environments are provided for ducks and other birds.

And on the western edge of the Great Swamp is the much smaller Lord Stirling Park with its Environmental Education Center. Here bird and nature watching are a somewhat easier proposition, as the center provides a large parking facility and easily accessible trails that start right there. Included in the park are some eight miles of marked walking trails, as well as a boardwalk especially designed for the handicapped and young children.

The center provides a wide variety of year-round seasonal activities for people of all ages. For example, in winter they feature winter search parties (to find out where insects go), discussions on hibernation, exploring the terrain on snowshoes, nature photography workshops, film and slide shows, owl prowls, marsh meanders, moonlight cross-country skiing, and maple sugaring. Throughout the year the center posts a wildlife sighting list in its headquarters, which indicates what animals and birds have been spotted recently and where they can be seen.

Walking in the Great Swamp trails (including Lord Stirling Park) is fairly easy because the land is generally flat. Anyone who is interested in nature and the environment, particularly in birds, will enjoy this special habitat. It's a fine place for a visit any time of the year, bearing in mind that migratory birds are best seen in spring and fall. In spring, summer, and early fall you will see masses of wildflowers throughout. Some 200 species of flowering plants are found here and are listed in a free booklet available at the center. As most birders know, for the most successful birding you should plan on arriving early in the morning or late in the afternoon. Bring along waterproof gear or sturdy shoes that can get wet. During the summer months it might be a good idea to bring insect repellent to ward off mosquitoes, ticks, and deer flies.

For further information, contact the refuge manager at 201-647-1222; or the Environmental Education Center at 201-766-2489.

THE WALK

The easier walk begins at the Environmental Center, where you can leave your car. Inside the headquarters you can get a number of free fliers that describe the variety of animal and plant life, as well as a list of current sightings. Among the birds you can expect to see (depending on the season) are the mallard and black duck, green heron, Canada goose, green-winged and blue-winged heron, hawk, sora, common snipe, yellow-billed and black-billed cuckoo, indigo bunting, blue-winged warbler, mourning dove, eastern screech-owl, red-winged blackbird, and various types of woodpecker, to name a few. If you're lucky you might see the blue-spotted salamander, a rare species found only here in all of New Jersey. There are many mammals in the region, including shrews, voles, beavers, occasional foxes, river otters, and long-tailed weasels. Some bear tracks were recently spotted, although bears are rarely observed in the refuge. The most common mammal to be found is the white-tailed deer, of which there are an estimated several hundred in number at the present time.

There are basically two marked trails within Lord Stirling Park, as well as the relatively short boardwalk described above. These trails begin near the headquarters, continue past the pretty pond area and into the woods. They are both loops, so that you don't have to retrace your steps.

If you prefer walking through the heart of the Great Swamp, we suggest you first drive to the refuge headquarters maintenance complex on Plains Road, past the south gate, a rather hostile-looking entrance with road spikes on one side to prevent people from exiting with their cars there. You can get information concerning where best to leave your car and start off from there. You can also get a map of the wilderness trail system as distinct from the more accessible and less forbidding Lord Stirling section. Remember not to park or stop your car except in designated spots within the refuge. The eastern section encompasses the wilderness area with its 8.5 miles of hiking trails. Parking space (with room for only a few cars) is found on the outer reaches of this area.

38

Bird Watching in a Shady Conifer Forest
Muttontown Nature Preserve, L.I.

HOW TO GET THERE:

Long Island Expressway to exit 41 north. Take Route 106 north to its intersection with Route 25A. Go left (west) a very short distance. When you reach the Howard Johnson (on your right), cross the highway to Muttontown Lane, which will take you right to the entrance.

Muttontown Nature Preserve consists of 550 acres of woodlands, fields, marshes, and a conifer stand, all prettily nestled on Long Island's North Shore. It's a spot we recommend for birders. Because of its variety of terrain, many different species of birds can be seen here all year. The preserve includes lands that were once country estates or farms, and that are now being allowed to return to their natural state. It also includes mature woodlands that have been in existence for generations. With its pleasantly winding (but mostly flat) trails through wooded land and field, it is an oasis of peace and quiet where the sounds you hear are those of its birds or the breeze through grassy fields or forests. Some of the trails were once bridle paths from the days when the region was dotted with elegant horse farms. (There are still quite a few. In fact, the visitor is likely to meet an occasional rider, as there are equestrian trails within the confines of the preserve.)

The birder or nature watcher has the choice of several well-marked trails, all of which are explained in maps and informative pamphlets on the birds, trees, wildflowers, mammals, reptiles, and amphibians that may be found at particular times of the year. These free materials are available at the nature center.

As in all bird watching, the best time to view birds is early in the morning or late in the day. Spring and fall—with their migrations—bring the greatest numbers, but there is plenty to see in summer and winter, too. In fact, winter is a fine time, as you can spot birds more easily without their being camouflaged by the foliage.

This is a surprisingly cool spot, recommended for hot days, for the great trees make it shady and it is close enough to the water to pick up ocean breezes. The walk is fairly easy; one that anyone can do. Take your usual birding gear. Remember not to: collect plants, minerals or animals, build fires, litter, or wander off trails. The preserve is open daily from 9:30 A.M. to 4:30 P.M. For further information, call 516-922-3123 or 922-2668.

THE WALK

After you have left your car at the parking area outside the nature center, enter the small building to gather whatever information interests you. We recommend you pick up a map of the preserve. There are also four separate brochures listing birds to be found at each season, as well as material on other animals and plants to identify.

The paths meander through several ecological environments, each of which is home to different species of plants and animals. Follow blue or green blazes through the moist woodsy swamplands, where red maples, pin oaks, and ferns proliferate. Here you will see warblers during spring and fall. In the fields you will find many wildflowers, as well as vines, shrubs, and tall grasses. Bob-whites and pheasants thrive in this habitat. The woodland area of relatively young trees—40 or 50 years old—has many white ash, dogwood, apple, red maple, black cherry, and white pine. In the particularly quiet and peaceful conifer stand, where eastern white pine and European larch were planted in the early part of the century, you might spot chickadees, kinglets, crossbills, pine siskins, and others. The rolling hills with their small ponds surrounded by persimmon trees attract populations of aquatic insects, amphibians, and reptiles. Finally, the mature woodlands of black oak, chestnut oak, black birch, and Norway spruce of mixed ages are the perfect habitat for many different birds, including woodpeckers, hawks, and owls. You can choose where you want to go, depending on what you wish to see.

In springtime, you might see the Canada goose, snow goose, mallard, mourning dove, crow, black-capped chickadee, robin, red-winged blackbird, grackle, starling, tree sparrow, and dark-eyed junco. Sometimes—although rarely—you might see the turkey vulture, merlin, peregrine falcon, purple martin, fish crow, winter wren, gray-cheeked thrush, vesper sparrow, and bobolink.

In summer, you will likely find bob-whites, ring-neck pheasants, blue jays, black-capped chickadees, catbirds, blue-winged warblers, yellowthroats, red-winged blackbirds, grackles, house finches, goldfinches, or chipping sparrows. On rare occasions you might spot the peregrine falcon, black-backed gull, Blackburnian warbler, or great egret.

In autumn, you may see the American robin, cedar waxwing, parula warbler, American crow, black-capped chickadee, song sparrow, starling, or Blackburnian warbler, among the many varieties that appear at that time. Less likely are the snipe, ring-billed gull, cowbird, yellow-throated vireo, or great black-backed gull, although some have been spotted in the past.

Finally, in winter, look for the Canada goose, bob-white, ring-necked pheasant, herring gull, mourning dove, blue jay, robin, starling, cardinal, evening grosbeak, tree sparrow, or song sparrow. If you're lucky you may even see rough-legged hawks, woodcocks, belted kingfishers, or white-winged crossbills.

Follow the well-marked trails, use your guides, and enjoy the birds!

AFTER THE WALK

You are near several major North Shore attractions: visit the Vanderbilt Mansion (see walk 13); the home and grounds of Teddy Roosevelt's Sagamore Hill (walk 15); or drive out to the beach and breakwater at Eaton's Neck (walk 16).

39

Birding in Jamaica Bay Wildlife Refuge
Queens, N.Y.

HOW TO GET THERE:

By subway: IND line (A train) to Broad Channel, then walk west to Cross Bay Boulevard and north .75 mile. By car, take the Long Island Expressway to Woodhaven Boulevard, which becomes Cross Bay Boulevard, which will go right into the area. Park at the headquarters, where you can also pick up information on the layout of the refuge.

Although this wonderful birding spot is technically in New York City, its astonishing array of birds makes it hard to believe its so-called urban location. It is directly across the bay from the John F. Kennedy Airport and in clear weather you can actually see the skyscrapers of Manhattan. But more than 250 species of birds are found here, including rare and uncommon species. So, although we have not included other city locations, we couldn't leave out Jamaica Bay for our birders and other walkers seeking interesting terrain.

Jamaica Bay Wildlife Refuge, part of the Gateway National Recreation Area, was formerly Jamaica Bay Park, a city park planted deliberately to suit the tastes of birds by a man named Herbert Johnson. Now it is administered by the federal government and is one of the most beloved birders' sites on the East Coast. Storm damage to trees and other plants is carefully repaired. The administration provides a lecture room, rest rooms, and an information desk. (No refreshments are available, no picnicking allowed, and of course no collecting or disturbing of the habitat.)

This extraordinary and unusual terrain includes a shrubby woodland, a grassy area called the North Garden, and a large area of marshes, a beach area (occasionally closed when birds are nesting), a freshwater pond, and many walks with observation points. This is a fine place for a full day's walking and observing.

The birds seen here include more than 50 varieties, among

JAMAICA BAY
WILDLIFE REFUGE

them the glossy ibis, the greater scaup, the hooded merganser, osprey, white-rumped sandpiper, roseate tern, summer tanager, the Lapland longspur, some rare warblers, and the European widgeon. You are more likely to spot egrets, ruddy ducks, white-crowned sparrows, snow geese, as well as robins, hermit thrushes, and Cape May warblers.

Fall and spring migratory birds are everywhere in Jamaica Bay, making it an excellent outing for birders. Rare winter birds include the peregrine falcon, the black-headed gull, and many seabirds. You can get more information on Jamaica Bay and its possibilities by writing to the Jamaica Bay Unit of the Gateway National Recreation Area, at Floyd Bennett Field, Brooklyn, N.Y. 11234, or by calling the New York Audubon Society at 212-691-7483, which can tell you what to look for at different times.

40

Birding in Rural Westchester
Ward Pound Ridge Reservation, Cross River, N.Y.

HOW TO GET THERE:

Major Deegan Expressway to Cross County Parkway to the Hutchinson River Parkway to Route 684 North to Route 35 (turn right). Stay on Route 35 until you come to the junction of Route 121 and follow signs to the reservation.

The Ward Pound Ridge Reservation is an ideal birding and hiking area for those seeking to combine a natural environment and bird habitat. This vast reservation—some 5,000 acres of woodland, open fields, swampland, ravines, and a hidden pond—is home or breeding ground to more than 100 species. It is situated within rural Westchester County on the border of Connecticut in a region of rolling hills, old stone walls, rustic homesteads, and wonderful country air. Even if you are not a birder we recommend this peaceful sanctuary for its 35 miles of scenic walking trails (including four self-guided trails) that provide a real respite from urban life. As you wander about you may cross paths with an occasional horseback rider—this is horse country—perhaps a cross-country skier or two on a crisp winter day, or another walker on a nature outing. The park is spacious and never feels crowded within its many winding trails, even on busy weekends.

The reservation has additional facilities that make it a good place for families with children. The Trailside Nature Museum, with its specimens of birds, mammals, reptiles, insects, minerals, as well as its well-regarded Delaware Indian Resource Center, is a good place to browse before or after your walk. Here you can also pick up information about the park: a map showing the trails, a calendar of park events, and a list of birds that have recently been sighted. The museum is open Wednesday through Sunday, 9:00 A.M. to 5:00 P.M., year round. Call 914-763-3993.

There are over two dozen rustic stone and wooden shelters for campers, some picnicking facilities, areas for sledding (far enough away from trails so as not to disturb birders and others seeking peace and quiet), and a charming .5 acre wildflower garden with 100 labeled varieties.

An outing to Ward Pound Ridge is recommended at any time of year, because of the birds that come here, even in winter. The terrain varies from somewhat hilly to fairly flat; it is not difficult for the average walker. There are restrictions: no hunting, no fires (except in designated areas), no unleashed pets, no collecting either minerals or plants, no capturing animals or trapping. Fishing is allowed in certain areas. Open all year from 9:00 A.M. to dusk. For information call 914-763-3493.

THE WALK

Leave your car (for a small fee, in season) in one of the designated areas; parking is not allowed along roadsides. If you're here on a day when the museum is open, go there first to pick up a map or a list of birds. Otherwise, you can get park information at the main office near the entrance.

The trails you choose and where you set off will depend in part on the types of habitats that interest you. Wetlands, hills, ponds, and rocky areas are marked on the map. In the wetlands, profuse with mosses, marsh marigolds, skunk cabbage, and blueberry bushes, you will see ducks and other waterfowl, as well as frogs and salamanders. Look for bluebirds near the large maple trees.

Other birds (depending on the season) include the Canada goose, northern harrier, sharp-shinned hawk, red-tailed hawk, ruffed grouse, rock dove, mourning dove, downy woodpecker, hairy woodpecker, northern flicker, horned lark, purple martin, cliff swallow, black-capped chickadee, tufted titmouse, golden-crowned kinglet, gray catbird, northern mockingbird, brown thrasher, cedar waxwing, European starling, blue-winged warbler, Tennessee warbler, Blackburnian warbler, ovenbird, common yellowthroat, rose-breasted grosbeak, song sparrow, swamp sparrow, common grackle, northern oriole, and house finch. Of course there are many birds that are spotted only occasionally or rarely. Among the rare species that have been seen here are the American bittern, American black duck, bald eagle, merlin, upland sandpiper, long-eared owl, northern saw-whet owl, olive-sided flycatcher, northern shrike, marsh wren, pine warbler, clay-colored sparrow, red crossbill, white-winged crossbill, and common redpoll.

OTHER BIRDING LOCATIONS NEARBY

There are several other bird-watching spots in Westchester, not far from the city, that bear mentioning. Among them are two that are administered by the Saw Mill River Audubon Society; both are in Chappaqua.

The Gedney Brook Sanctuary consists of some 60 acres of swampland, ridge, and rocky landscape. This preserve is particularly noted for its woodpeckers, but there are many other varieties to be seen. Since there is much wet and marshy land in this sanctuary, you'll find quite a few water birds, including wood ducks, mallards, and spotted sandpipers.

The other preserve, quite nearby, is the Pinecliff Sanctuary. This one also has a special conservation aim: preserving wetlands and the species of wildlife that enjoy them. This is a small sanctuary of just about 7 acres, but you'll find a wide variety of pond life to watch, including toads, frogs, salamanders, dragonflies, etc. Birds spotted here include crested flycatchers in spring.

41

Birding in the Marshland Conservancy
Rye, N.Y.

HOW TO GET THERE:

From George Washington Bridge, take Cross Bronx Expressway, then take the Bruckner Expressway to Route 95, to exit 18B (Mamaroneck Avenue), bear right and take a left onto Route 1. Entrance to the Conservancy is on your right.

The Marshland Conservancy is a nice spot for birding and walking in close proximity to the city. Surrounded by elegant and imposing mansions with columned facades, it once was the private estate of John Jay, the first Chief Justice of the U.S., and is now a preserve owned and operated by the County of Westchester. This rural tract of land includes a great variety of habitats—woodlands, marshes, mud flats, and a nice big field—that provide a haven for all kinds of birds and other animals. It is an appealing, scenic spot, where you can walk through the quiet woods, view seashore marshes with tall grasses from a panoramic lookout, or meander across the vast, open field. The preserve is refreshing in its simplicity: there are few signs of organized activity, few do's and don'ts. It's simply a place for quiet observation, where you can watch birds and other animals unhampered by outside interruptions.

There is a small, discreet museum with exhibits of local plants and animals, as well as a couple of pleasing trails that circle through the woods and fields, where you might spot an occasional pheasant or even a great horned owl.

This is a good place to visit throughout the year, as there is always something of interest. The field, which was once a wheat field and is now left alone with only occasional tending, is filled with varieties of wildflowers. In summer it is ablaze with orange butterfly weed; in early fall, it becomes a mass of yellow, with its profusion of goldenrod and sunflowers.

THE WALK

Leave your car at the small parking area next to the shelter. You have a choice of a couple of interconnecting trails that wander through the woods, alongside and into the fields, eventually leading you to the overlook with its dramatic view onto the marshes and Milton Harbor below. You can continue your walk, going down to the marsh, on the beach alongside the bay, and out to a neck called Marie's Neck, for another scenic panoramic view. (Watch out for poison ivy!)

This rich habitat attracts all kinds of animals. The marsh grasses provide food for crabs, mussels, clams, snails, and other animals that in turn attract such birds as snowy and great egrets, great blue herons, and both black-and yellow-crowned herons. In fact, this is considered one of the best places on the nearby shore to view these varieties of wildlife. Along the seashore you can expect to see many different kinds of ducks, as well as herring, great black-backed and ring-billed gulls. Along the beach look for horseshoe crabs, particularly in late May and early June, when they lay their eggs.

42

Rambling and Birding in Connecticut
Audubon Center, Greenwich
Larsen Sanctuary, Fairfield
Devil's Den, Weston

HOW TO GET THERE:

The Audubon Center in Greenwich: The center is located at 613 Riversville Road, Greenwich, but it is nearer to Armonk, N.Y., than downtown Greenwich. From New York take the West Side Highway or Major Deegan to Cross County Parkway, to Hutchinson River Parkway, which runs into the Merritt Parkway. Take exit 28. Go north for 1.4 miles. Take John Street. Riversville Road is 1.4 miles farther.

The Larsen Sanctuary: Follow above directions to the Merritt Parkway, take exit 44, and turn right immediately at the bottom of the ramp, onto Congress Street. At the first stop-light take a right onto Burr Street. The center is about 1 mile down the road, on the left.

Devil's Den in Weston: Follow above directions to Merritt Parkway. Take exit 42, go north on CT 57 for five miles. Turn right on Godfrey Road, and then left on Pent Road.

The following three bird walks are all in nearby Connecticut. Each has a slightly different ambiance, but all are especially nice outings for just plain walkers, as well as for bird watchers. Of course, migrating season (spring and fall) is best for seeing birds. However, we recommend these walks year-round (except on slippery ice or snow) because the scenery in each will give you a fine taste of Connecticut countryside, with its hidden ponds and lakes, its tall trees, giant boulders, and old stone walls. While there are many other sanctuaries in the western part of the state, we think these three are among the nicest.

You can telephone the numbers given below to find out what birds are being spotted at any given time. A checklist is also

THREE BIRDING SITES IN CONNECTICUT

available at the Audubon headquarters at the Greenwich and Larsen sites. Though experts tell us that birds are fewer in Connecticut than they used to be, there are still plenty to be sighted. Take your binoculars and your walking shoes! Leave dogs (even leashed) at home.

AUDUBON CENTER IN GREENWICH

These woodsy 477 acres have both rocky forest paths and a hidden lake (Lake Mead) deep within the preserve. The quiet of the countryside is broken only by bird calls; when we were there it was very uncrowded and the pristine stillness was perfect for bird watching. About 190 species have been seen here; 87 of them nesting. There are field, thicket, lake, swamp, stream, and orchard habitats, as well as a self-guiding trail. Remains of stone walls from earlier farming days—for which New England is so well known—add to the interest of the walk, and there are varieties of indigenous trees, mushrooms, wildflowers, turtles, frogs, and other wildlife.

The forest walk was very pretty in the autumn, with the sun filtering through bright tree leaves, but it was the lake and its rocky path and dam to walk across that were particularly striking. The colors of the foliage reflected in the lake made a wonderful background for viewing birds as they came to dip in the lake. There are two wonderful bird blinds on the edges of the lake; tall wooden towers with rustic seats and lookout space allowed us to prop binoculars on the sill and stare silently and unseen at the still water and the swooping birds.

Different seasons, of course, bring different birds. Among the nesting species to be found here are the green heron, Canada goose, ruby-throated hummingbird, four kinds of woodpeckers, and 14 kinds of warblers. In fact, warblers seen here include some of the most uncommon species seen in the Northeast. Cedar waxwings, flycatchers, vireos, and (rarely) the eastern bluebird and Philadelphia vireo have been sighted. The center recommends May for best birding (warblers especially), but other seasons are also rewarding. In October there is a hawk watch, as well as various other specific events for birders: natural history walks, trail hikes, watches for particular birds, and ecology workshops. A trail guide booklet is available that describes each habitat, includes a map, and also provides a checklist of birds.

The walk in this Audubon Center is rather hilly, but the footing is clearly marked and easy, over soft pine-needled paths. We do not recommend it for those who dislike a bit of a climb, although some of the paths are on a grassy knoll at the top. But if you have enough stamina not to puff going up a hill or two, it's a pleasant place for a birder's outing. For further information, call 203-869-5272.

LARSEN SANCTUARY IN FAIRFIELD

This 170-acre preserve is another Audubon sanctuary. The center located here is surrounded by 6.5 miles of trails in a gentle wilderness area.

There is a woodchip-lined path that takes the walker through forest, ponds, and swampland. Particularly resplendent in autumn when the maples and other trees are at their brilliant best, this sanctuary reminds us of what Connecticut must have looked like before the villages and suburbs grew up.

Among the many birds sighted here are woodpeckers, whose workmanship can be spotted, barn and tree swallows, mourning doves, American goldfinches, and ruby-throated hummingbirds. Other visitors to the area include cedar waxwings, migrating warblers, nuthatches, mockingbirds, belted kingfishers, kinglets, grosbeaks, swamp sparrows, and starlings. The center gives out a complete list for checking and will tell you what to look for at any particular time.

Among the most interesting features of this walk are the wood duck boxes sitting on poles in the middle of the pond. These boxes allow wood ducks to nest, and birders can be well rewarded at seeing them. The best seasons for visiting this center are, of course, migrating time (spring and fall); but it is open year round, and the visitor will find birds of interest at any time.

The center has an added attraction for the blind and handicapped. A "singing and fragrance walk" begins near the parking area. This is a smooth path with a wooden railing that allows visitors to walk through heavily scented bushes and flowers and listen to various bird calls. Since much of birding involves listening rather than seeing, this trail seems like a wonderful idea, and the center has done a good job with it.

The Larsen Sanctuary is open from 9:00 A.M. to 4:30 P.M. Tuesday through Saturday and noon to 4:30 P.M. on Sunday. The grounds are open all the time, year round.

DEVIL'S DEN IN THE LUCIUS POND ORDWAY PRESERVE, WESTON

This is one of the prettiest walks we have taken. The sight of the lake, when we came upon it, hidden away in the woods, with the trees reflected brilliantly on the still surface, brought to mind Impressionist paintings. The natural hilliness of the landscape, the bits of old stone walls and fallen tree limbs, the rushing water over the dam where once Colonial millers worked were all especially appealing. And in addition there are birds! Instead of the carefully arranged habitats in so many nature preserves, we found Devil's Den wonderfully underdeveloped. (Though there are a few signs giving details about an old charcoal oven and the dam.)

Devil's Den gets its name from hoofprint-shaped marks that were found on some of the rocks. Turn-of-the-century charcoal makers believed these prints were made by the devil's hot feet! We saw neither the marks nor the devil, but we did spot a variety of interesting trees, birds, frogs, and other wildlife. Devil's Den includes 1,540 acres, with approximately 20 miles of trails. A map is obtainable at the entrance from a small wooden box, where you can also sign in. There is great variety in this large area, and the map will help you choose among woods, pond, swamp, and the beautiful lakeside trail.

The lake draws a large variety of waterfowl, including the heron, Canada goose, mallard duck, and osprey. Among the other birds sighted at Devil's Den are the sharp-shinned hawk, ruffed grouse, woodcock, mourning dove, chimney swift, slate-colored junco, belted kingfisher, scarlet tanager, several kinds of woodpecker, and the familiar jays, crows, chickadees, and robins. Rarer visitors are the thrush, red-winged blackbird, towhee, swamp sparrow, yellow-billed cuckoo, and the great horned owl.

Walking around Devil's Den is fairly easy. The trails we took were well marked, soft under foot, and carefully constructed over obstacles. In fact, plank bridges across streams and small gorges are covered with chicken wire to keep walkers from slipping. The many large boulders of the Connecticut landscape provide nice resting spots, particularly on the banks of the lake.

There is no fee, and the preserve is open from dawn to dusk. Devil's Den suggests telephoning (203-226-4991) for a permit, but you may register on the day of your hike. We arrived and walked through without ever spotting another soul, including anyone to issue us a permit. Devil's Den belongs to The Nature Conservancy, a national nonprofit environmental organization that has been in existence since 1951. The areas owned by this group include 2.5 million acres of natural lands in our hemisphere; volunteers staff most areas. Devil's Den will be happy to have you join the conservancy, and you can receive the right to a yearly permit.

CHOOSING AN OUTING

An Interest in Art

Village Walks

Preserves and Sanctuaries

Great Swamp, N.J. (nature) — Walk 37
Litchfield, Conn. (historic village) — Walk 29
Mianus River Gorge Wildlife and Botanical Preserve, N.Y. (nature) — Walk 19
Mushroom Forays, N.J. — Walk 3
Planting Fields Arboretum, L.I. (garden) — Walk 14
Princeton University, N.J. (campus) — Walk 10
Sagamore Hill, L.I. (estate) — Walk 15
Sandy Hook, N.J. (nature) — Walk 35
Scherman-Hoffman Audubon Center, N.J. (nature) — Walk 36
Sleepy Hollow Cemetery, N.Y. — Walk 18
Sleepy Hollow Restorations, N.Y. — Walk 18
Storm King Art Center, N.Y. (sculpture) — Walk 24
Tewksbury Wine Cellars, N.J. (vineyard) — Walk 5
Vanderbilt Museum, L.I. (historic estate/natural history)—tour required — Walk 13
West Point Military Academy, N.Y. (military site) — Walk 24

Enjoying Fall Foliage

Applewood Orchards, N.Y. — Walk 27
Cold Spring, N.Y. — Walk 20
Croton, N.Y. — Walk 17
Hope, N.J. — Walk 9
Kaaterskill Falls, N.Y. — Walk 22
Litchfield, Conn. — Walk 29
Putnam Memorial State Park, Conn. — Walk 30
Rockefeller State Park Preserve, N.Y. — Walk 21
Storm King Art Center, N.Y. — Walk 24

Cold Weather and Off Season Outings (Including Indoors)

Caumsett State Park, L.I. — Walk 12
Doris Duke Gardens, N.J. — Walk 4
Mianus River Gorge Wildlife and Botanical Preserve, N.Y. — Walk 19
Nyack Beach State Park, N.Y. — Walk 28
Piermont, N.Y. — Walk 25
Planting Fields Arboretum, L.I. — Walk 14
Princeton University, N.J. — Walk 10
Rockefeller State Park Preserve, N.Y. — Walk 21
Rockland Lake, N.Y. — Walk 23
Sagamore Hill, N.Y. — Walk 15
Sandy Hook, N.J. — Walk 35
Vanderbilt Museum, L.I. — Walk 13

Fruits, Vegetables, Mushrooms, and Wine

Applewood Orchard, N.Y. — Walk 27
Bowman's Hill State Wildflower Preserve and Medicinal Trail, Pa. — Walk 32, 33
Cheesequake State Park, N.J. (mushroom hunting) — Walk 3
Haight Vineyards & Winery, Conn. — Walk 29
Jenny Jump State Forest, N.J. (mushroom hunting) — Walk 3
Matarazzo Farms, N.J. (vegetable and fruit farm) — Walk 3

Mianus River Gorge Wildlife and Botanical Preserve, N.Y. (mushroom   Walk 19
   hunting)
Planting Fields Arboretum, L.I. (herbarium)   Walk 14
Race Farm, N.J. (apple orchard)   Walk 9
Stokes State Forest, N.J. (mushroom hunting)   Walk 3
Tewksbury Wine Cellars, N.J.   Walk 5

Crafty Outings

Allaire Abandoned Village, N.J. (crafts exhibits)   Walk 1
Fairfield Old Burying Ground, Conn. (grave rubbings)   Walk 31
Garrison, N.Y. (pottery making)   Walk 20
Museum Village of Orange County, N.Y. (craft demonstrations)   Walk 27
New Hope, Pa. (craft/antique shops)   Walk 34
Nyack, N.Y. (craft/antique shops)   Walk 28
Oldwick Zion Evangelical Lutheran Church, N.J. (grave rubbings)   Walk 5
Sleepy Hollow Cemetery (grave rubbings), N.Y.   Walk 18
Sleepy Hollow Restorations, N.Y. (colonial crafts/demonstrations)   Walk 18
Sugar Loaf, N.Y. (crafts in progress)   Walk 27
United House Wreckers, Conn. (for collectors)   Walk 31

Gardens, Indoors and Out

Bowman's Hill State Wildlife Preserve   Walk 32
Bowman's Hill State Wildlife Preserve Medicinal Trail, Pa.   Walk 33
Colonial Park Fragrance and Sensory Garden, N.J.   Walk 11
Doris Duke Gardens, N.J.   Walk 4
Planting Fields Arboretum, L.I.   Walk 14
Ward Pound Ridge Reservation wildflower garden, N.Y.   Walk 40

Special Provisions for the Handicapped

Bowman's Hill State Wildflower Preserve, Pa.   Walk 33
Caramoor, N.Y.   Walk 19
Colonial Park, N.J.   Walk 11
Great Swamp (Lord Stirling Park), N.J.   Walk 37
Larsen Sanctuary, Conn. (singing and fragrance walk)   Walk 42
Vanderbilt Planetarium, L.I.   Walk 13

Nature Centers and Interpretative Trails

Audubon Center, Greenwich, Conn.   Walk 42
Bowman's Hill State Wildflower Preserve and Medicinal Trail, Pa.   Walk 32, 33
Great Swamp, N.J.   Walk 37
Mianus River Gorge Wildlife and Botanical Preserve, N.Y.   Walk 19
Rockland Lake, N.Y.   Walk 23
Scherman-Hoffman Audubon Center, N.J.   Walk 36
Vanderbilt Museum (fish and other animals), L.I.   Walk 13
Ward Pound Ridge Reservation, N.Y.   Walk 40
White Memorial Foundation and Litchfield Nature Center, Conn.   Walk 29

Famous Houses and Interesting Estates

"Boscobel," N.Y.	Walk 20
"Caramoor," N.Y.	Walk 19
Frederick Church's "Olana," N.Y.	Walk 22
De Windt House, N.Y.	Walk 25
Jay Gould's "Lyndhurst," N.Y.	Walk 18
Homes of Harriet Beecher Stowe, Ethan Allan, and Henry Ward Beecher, Conn.	Walk 29
Homes of Woodrow Wilson, Albert Einstein, Paul Robeson, and Thomas Mann, N.J.	Walk 10
Edward Hopper House, N.Y.	Walk 28
Washington Irving's "Sunnyside," N.Y.	Walk 18
John Jay Homestead, N.Y.	Walk 19
"Morven," home of N.J. governors	Walk 10
Teddy Roosevelt's "Sagamore Hill," L.I.	Walk 15
William K. Vanderbilt, Vanderbilt Museum, L.I.	Walk 13

Waterfronts, Waterfalls, and Seashores

Caumsett State Park, L.I.	Walk 12
Cold Spring, N.Y.	Walk 20
Croton Dam, N.Y.	Walk 17
Devil's Den, Conn.	Walk 42
Eaton's Neck, L.I.	Walk 16
Harriman State Park, N.Y.	Walk 26
Jones Road Park, N.J.	Walk 6
Kaaterskill Falls, N.Y.	Walk 22
Mianus River Gorge Wildlife and Botanical Preserve, N.Y.	Walk 19
New Hope Canal, Pa.	Walk 34
Nyack Beach State Park, N.Y.	Walk 28
Ocean Grove, N.J.	Walk 7
Palisades Shore Walk, N.J.	Walk 2
Piermont, N.Y.	Walk 25
Rockefeller State Park Preserve, N.Y.	Walk 21
Rockland Lake, N.Y.	Walk 23
Sandy Hook, N.J.	Walk 35
Southport, Conn.	Walk 31

Walks for the Fittest

Cold Spring, N.Y. (Washburn Trail)	Walk 20
Fitness Trail, N.J.	Walk 8
Great Swamp, N.J.	Walk 37
Harriman State Park, N.Y.	Walk 26
Kaaterskill Falls, N.Y.	Walk 22
Mianus River Gorge Wildlife and Botanical Preserve, N.Y.	Walk 19

Of Interest to Children